Pentecost

The Sanctioning of the Apostles

By
Steven A. Carlson

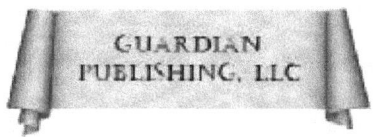

Copyright © 2010, Steven A. Carlson
All Rights Reserved
ISBN: 978-0-9827915-4-7
Printed in the United States of America

This edition published in November 2010 in association with

Guardian Publishing, LLC
Holt, Michigan

guardianpublishingllc.com

All Scripture quotations, unless otherwise noted, are taken from the Holy Bible: New American Standard Bible (NASB), Copyright © 2002. Used by permission of the Zondervan Corporation, all rights reserved. Occasionally other versions are cited, especially to denote the contrast in translations by various interpreters. These versions include the American Standard Version (ASV), Amplified Version (AV), King James Version (KJV), The Message, New International Version (NIV), New King James Version (NKJV), and the New Revised Standard Version (NRSV).

All rights reserved. No part of this publication may be reproduced, stored in a retrieval system, or transmitted in any form or by any means – electronic, mechanical, photocopying, recording, or any other – except for brief quotations in printed reviews, without the prior written permission of the publisher.

Other books by Steven A. Carlson:

Baptism and the Battle for Souls
Faith That Demands Obedience

Baptism and the Plan of Salvation
Restoring the New Testament Gospel

Born of Water and the Spirit
Entering the Kingdom

Christian Principles: Raising the Bar
Engaging Lessons from the Sermon on the Mount

One Bible...And Yet, So Many Beliefs
Exploring the Doctrinal Chaos

Acknowledgements

I would like to dedicate this book to my parents, Elton and Edna Carlson, who passed away in 2009. My father was a minister who spent over sixty years in the preaching ministry. While we often discussed his retirement, it eventually became obvious that it was a pipe dream on my part. His ministry and the opportunity to preach the Word of God meant more to him than pretty much anything else in the world. He was probably with us for so long because he was able to continue serving God in that capacity.

My mother was by his side through that entire ministry, preceding him in death by a mere six months. While she was the dutiful wife, she was well-studied herself. At her graveside, I commented that the apostle John was no doubt receiving insights at that time from my mother concerning the book of Revelation.

Living their lives in the ministry, my parents left very few physical assets behind. They were never wealthy as men count wealth, but then they tended to concentrate on things above. Worldly goods did not hold a lot of meaning for them. However, what they did leave me is a legacy more valuable than silver or gold. Although we did not agree on every detail of Scripture, they taught me to (1) approach God's Word honestly and (2) never simply take someone else's word concerning what is acceptable doctrine.

They encouraged me to dive into the words of Scripture to honestly determine what the authors said rather than relying on the questionable interpretations of men. Their guidance has helped me to recognize deficient biblical teaching on numerous occasions and is probably what has led to a writing style that leaves no stone unturned when determining scriptural truth. That is the best thing they could have done for me and I am grateful beyond words. Thanks, Mom and Dad.

I am deeply indebted to my ever-faithful editing/proofreading team consisting of my three children, Michael, Adam, and Crystal Carlson, along with an unofficially adopted daughter by the name of Annette Bobko. I have become quite comfortable placing my work in their hands, knowing that it will return to me significantly improved.

I would also like to thank my wife Denise for showing remarkable patience and understanding over my choice to become a writer. She has always fully supported me in my career and in my role as an elder in the church. Now she has gone beyond the call of duty in allowing me to fulfill the dream of writing.

Finally, I must thank my brother, Tim Carlson, who is a minister and whose grasp of Scripture and apostolic doctrine exceeds my own. He has been an exceptionally valuable asset throughout my labors as an author, happily providing me with biblical insights I otherwise might have missed. Having his support and deep biblical knowledge in my corner has buoyed my confidence as an author and helped to ensure the thoroughness and scriptural integrity of the message that is conveyed within these pages. Thanks a lot, Tim.

Table of Contents

Title	Page
Preface	8
Chapter 1: The Promise to the Apostles - Acts 1: 1-8	11
Chapter 2: The Ascension - Acts 1: 9-11	16
Chapter 3: The Return to Jerusalem - Acts 1: 12-14	19
Chapter 4: The Selection of Matthias - Acts 1: 15-26	24
Chapter 5: The Holy Spirit - Acts 2: 1-4	32
Chapter 6: The Crowd - Acts 2: 5-13	43
Chapter 7: The Fulfillment of Prophecy - Acts 2: 14-21	51
Chapter 8: The Message - Acts 2: 22-36	56
Chapter 9: The Response - Acts 2: 37-41	63
Chapter 10: The Aftermath - Acts 2: 42-47	71
Chapter 11: Baptism	78
Chapter 12: Spiritual Gifts	83
Conclusion	89
Bibliography	92

Preface

The apostles cautioned the first century Christians to beware of men who distort Scripture and, as a consequence, teach doctrinal views that conflict with God's Word. In his letter to the Galatians, Paul warned about the existence of false gospels (Galatians 1: 6-7). He noted that any such *gospel* is really no gospel at all since God had only authorized one message of salvation. Paul was so adamant concerning the truth of the gospel that he directed his readers to ignore any message that conflicted with the gospel they had already received, even if that message was delivered by an angel of the Lord or one of the apostles, including Paul himself. He stated that anyone who presented a false gospel would be accursed, repeating himself to make his point clear:

> [8] But even if we, or an angel from heaven, should preach to you a gospel contrary to what we have preached to you, he is to be accursed! [9] As we have said before, even now I say again: if anyone is preaching to you a gospel contrary to what you received, he is to be accursed! (Galatians 1: 8-9)

Peter wrote about men who would consciously choose to misrepresent scriptural instructions (2 Peter 3: 16-17). He considered these men to be untaught, unstable, and unprincipled, admonishing his readers to distance themselves from this kind of divisiveness. Peter wanted the early Christians to avoid being *carried away* [from Christ] by false teachers and, instead, remain faithful to the teachings of the apostles.

John addressed, in a direct fashion, certain men who had infiltrated the church with counterfeit views of Jesus' identity as the Son of God (1 John 2: 18-19). These men, known as Gnostics, were challenging the faith of believers in the late first century by denying the divine incarnation and certain other truths concerning the Messiah. John was passionate in his rebuke of these men, warning the disciples to refuse to entertain their heretical ideas. According to the apostle, one who welcomed false prophets and their teachings with open arms would be considered an active participant in their evil deeds (2 John 1: 7-11).

Dissension among early believers with respect to doctrine was a challenge for the evangelists of the first century. In his second letter to Timothy, the apostle Paul addressed the fact that this young minister of the faith may encounter those who, while proclaiming belief in Jesus, would dispute the principles set forth by the apostles. Their defiance would lead them to seek out spiritual counselors eager to teach them what they want to hear:

> [3] For *the* time will come when they will not tolerate sound doctrine; but *wanting* to have their ears tickled, they will accumulate for themselves teachers in accordance with their own desires, [4] and they will turn their ears away from the truth and will turn aside to myths. (2 Timothy 4: 3-4)

The apostles' words demonstrate their high regard for doctrinal integrity. They were unwavering when it came to apostolic truth and the proper presentation of the gospel message, portraying those who turned away from the apostles' instructions as *outside of Christ* due to their tainted views. Both Peter and Paul challenged the standing of those men and women who failed to obey the gospel message (2 Thessalonians 1: 7-9; 1 Peter 4: 17).

The apostles placed considerable emphasis on doctrinal purity. Yet, in modern times many have sought to trivialize the significance of biblical doctrine in man's relationship with God. It is not uncommon for men to contend that essentially *any* belief in God and/or Jesus is sufficient to receive an eternal reward, despite the words of Peter, Paul, and John.

While there are instances in Jesus' life, as it is revealed in the gospels, about which Bible scholars disagree, the vast majority of doctrinal disputes have arisen from teachings and events found in the New Testament epistles and the book of Acts. The doctrinal differences that tend to divide believers are a result of the numerous methods and/or preconceptions men employ when studying God's Word. Conflicting beliefs most often develop because someone has decided to ignore what Scripture teaches in favor of some other view that simply seems more appealing.

The book of Acts, located after the books of gospel and before the epistles in the New Testament, serves as an introduction to the early church through the work of the apostles. Given the content and placement of this book, it is fair to say that the events depicted in this historical look into the first century church are intended to set the stage for the balance of New Testament teachings.

Chronologically, as we move beyond Jesus' physical life here on earth (post-ascension), the first significant occasion we encounter in Scripture is the Day of Pentecost. The story of Pentecost is told in the second chapter of the book of Acts. Supplementing that narrative are the events of the first chapter of Acts that serve as a prelude, providing additional insight into that special day.

On the Day of Pentecost, the apostles were set aside, in an extraordinary manner, for the work of establishing the kingdom of God on earth. On that day, through the work of the Holy Spirit and the apostles, the church was born. However, much of the discord that has led to various doctrines and denominations stems from a misunderstanding of the details of Pentecost by very well-meaning individuals, which has resulted in a multitude of conflicting beliefs among men.

Given the fact that much doctrinal controversy begins with Pentecost, this work seeks to help the reader break through some of the confusion that has divided men over the centuries. With that goal in mind, we will reconsider what happened on that day, according to Scripture, and reflect on how those events affect the nature of the church and the balance of the inspired lessons taught by the apostles.

While the apostles were set aside on that day, Pentecost involved much more than the sanctioning of these twelve men. In a thorough examination of the first two chapters of the book of Acts, we will discover fulfillment of prophecy, the initial proclamation of the gospel message, and a portrait of the early church here on earth. There is clearly much to learn from the events of the day.

Chapter 1

The Promise to the Apostles

Acts 1: 1-8

¹ The first account I composed, Theophilus, about all that Jesus began to do and teach,

Luke, the author of the book of Acts, also penned the gospel of Luke. Both were written to the same person – a man named Theophilus – who appears to have been a friend of the author. However, we do not know the exact nature of their relationship. There is much speculation about the mysterious Theophilus, but his identity is unrelated to our purpose here. It is Luke's narrative that deserves our attention.

What we can take from this introduction to the book of Acts is the connection to Luke's first work. Luke wrote the book of Acts because he believed his mission was not completed when he finished the gospel of Luke. While Luke's gospel had revealed Jesus' life and ministry, much occurred after his ascension to heaven that needed to be shared.

The book of Acts, then, is Luke's continuation of the historical account that began with his gospel letter to Theophilus. He wanted to finish what he had started. Since, prior to his ascension, Jesus had left instructions for the apostles, Luke felt compelled to relate exactly how those commands, along with their accompanying promises, eventually manifested themselves.

² until the day when He was taken up *to heaven*, after He had given orders by the Holy Spirit to the apostles whom He had chosen.

Luke noted that the apostles received instructions, or commands, from Jesus prior to his ascension. Many of these instructions were given to the apostles over the course of time between the resurrection and ascension. These men had been personally selected by Jesus to fulfill the task at hand, which was to oversee the establishment of the kingdom of heaven on earth. Therefore, he had much to say to prepare them for what was ahead.

> ³ To these He also presented Himself alive after His suffering, by many convincing proofs, appearing to them over *a period of* forty days and speaking of things regarding the kingdom of God.

According to Luke, Jesus presented himself to the apostles after his resurrection. He used the pronoun *these*[1] to reference the apostles who were mentioned in the previous verse. Jesus appeared to a great number of the disciples between the time of his resurrection and his ascension. According to the apostle Paul, he even revealed himself to five hundred disciples at one time during this period while in Galilee (1 Corinthians 15: 6). In this early section of Acts, however, Luke focuses on Jesus' interaction with the apostles during that time. Jesus had been meeting with the apostles since the time of his resurrection, taking the opportunity to instruct them more fully about the kingdom of God. Luke recounts some of Jesus' contact with them in the first few verses of the book.

> ⁴ Gathering them together, He commanded them not to leave Jerusalem, but to wait for what the Father had promised, "Which," *He said*, "you heard of from Me; ⁵ for John baptized with water, but you will be baptized with the Holy Spirit not many days from now."

The encounter between Jesus and the apostles that is depicted in these verses is probably not at the Mount of Olives, but somewhere in Jerusalem, since another assembly occurs in verse six that appears to be the gathering for the ascenoun. There is speculation that at this time they were together for some kind of meal, but we cannot be certain.

Jesus told the apostles, on this occasion, to wait in Jerusalem for a short time. From the text, it appears that they were not told exactly how long they were to wait, but Jesus' words suggested that it would not be long. At the end of their wait, according to Jesus, they would "be baptized with the Holy Spirit." Jesus had previously promised these men that the Holy Spirit would come (John 14: 16-17; 15: 26; 16: 7-14). What is unclear from his remarks, however, is whether baptism with the Spirit would be limited to the apostles.

Only the apostles were present when Jesus spoke these words, but there was a time when John the Baptist prophesied concerning *baptism with the Spirit* in a more general setting (Matthew 3: 11). John the Baptist's prophecy was not only given to a crowd of people, but it was offered prior to Jesus' selection of those men who would eventually

---

[1] *To them* (NRSV); *to these men* (NIV); *to whom* (KJV; NKJV).

become apostles. Therefore, we have no reason to believe they were part of John's audience at the time, making it a prophecy to the general public.

Complementing the words of John the Baptist, Paul told the Corinthians that all members of the church body entered that body via the Holy Spirit (1 Corinthians 12: 13). Similarly, Jesus told Nicodemus that, "Unless one is born of water and the Spirit, he cannot enter into the kingdom of God" (John 3: 5). We can determine from these teachings that receiving the Spirit is something to be anticipated by more than the apostles. In fact, we can deduce from these other biblical passages that anyone who seeks to follow Jesus' teaching has an equal opportunity to receive the Spirit.

Baptism with the Holy Spirit, on this occasion as well as in the prophecy of John the Baptist, is measured against baptism with water. This suggests that baptism with the Holy Spirit would differ from the baptism in water with which they were so familiar. On Jesus' behalf the apostles had baptized many people in water as part of their ministry (John 3: 22; 4: 1-3). Now something different and new could be anticipated. Yet the apostles may not have known *how* it would differ and whether that difference would be physical, spiritual, or both.

God's Word does not offer a precise definition of the term *baptized with the Spirit*. Making the discussion even more challenging is the fact that in the New Testament, men are depicted receiving the Spirit by various means. For instance, on the Day of Pentecost (Acts 2: 4) and later, in Caesarea at the house of Cornelius (Acts 10: 44-46), the Spirit unexpectedly *fell upon* certain individuals, an experience that was accompanied by the physical manifestation of speaking in tongues. However, in the region known as Samaria (Acts 8: 14-18), and also at Ephesus (Acts 19: 6), men did not receive various spiritual gifts, and the Spirit did not *fall upon* them, until the apostles laid their hands on them. Finally, during Peter's sermon on the Day of Pentecost, he promised men what he termed the *gift* (or indwelling) of the Spirit (Acts 2: 38), which describes still another form of men receiving the Holy Spirit. The teaching concerning the inner presence of the Spirit, as promised by Peter, is sustained by Paul and John in their writings (Romans 8: 15; 1 Corinthians 6: 19; Ephesians 1: 13-14; 1 John 3: 24).

Given these numerous examples of how the Spirit interacted with men in the first century, it is easy to see why the expression *baptized with the Holy Spirit* remains a source of doctrinal diversity. A more in-depth discussion concerning this phrase will take place when we review the events of the Day of Pentecost. For now, we must recognize that on the day discussed in these verses, Jesus promised the apostles that they would "be baptized with the Holy Spirit" in a few days.

> ⁶ So, when they had come together, they *began* asking Him, saying, "Lord, is it at this time that You are restoring the kingdom to Israel?" ⁷ But He said to them, "It is not for you to know periods of time or appointed times which the Father has set by His own authority;

Luke's gospel concludes with Jesus' ascension to heaven in the presence of the apostles at the Mount of Olives (Luke 24: 50-53). While the gospel account of the ascension could be interpreted to suggest that more than the apostles were present at the ascension, since other disciples had been with them earlier in Jerusalem (Luke 24: 33), in these verses from the beginning of Acts, Luke offers supplementary information clarifying that only the apostles were present. In the narrative, the apostles are singled out over the course of several verses, leaving no room for doubt. The only available antecedents for the word *they* (v. 6) are Jesus and the apostles (v. 2).

We are offered only glimpses into the days between Jesus' resurrection and the ascension (Matthew 28: 1-20; Mark 16: 1-20; Luke 24: 1-50; John 20: 1 – 21: 25), but when Jesus revealed himself during this juncture it was normally in the presence of the apostles. After all, he had much to teach them about the kingdom of God if they were to carry on in his absence. As we consider Jesus' final moments on earth, we find that he spent the time with the apostles as he shared some final words with them before his departure.

When the apostles met with Jesus for what would prove to be their final contact with him on earth, they reverted to their old ways despite the abundance of teaching they had received. They still anticipated an earthly kingdom, asking if Jesus would now restore Israel to its rightful place as a nation, even though he had previously explained that the kingdom of God was spiritual in nature (Matthew 16: 28; Luke 17: 20-21; John 4: 23-24). Jesus rebuked them mildly, although he was probably exasperated by the query. He answered them by explaining something that should have been obvious to them: God's timing was not their concern. His answer reflected the fact that Jesus was more concerned with things that were relevant to the task that would soon be upon them – establishing the kingdom of God on earth.

⁸ but you will receive power when the Holy Spirit has come upon you; and you shall be My witnesses both in Jerusalem and in all Judea, and Samaria, and as far as the remotest part of the earth."

Just prior to his ascension, Jesus added a new dimension to his earlier discussion of the Holy Spirit. He explained to the apostles that when they received the Holy Spirit (it appears that he is discussing baptism with the Holy Spirit as discussed in verse five) they would also "receive power."

It is significant to note that this promise of power is specific to the apostles. Baptism with the Holy Spirit was promised on a larger scale in other settings, but the power mentioned here was promised in this setting alone. These words were spoken only to the apostles and only on this occasion. John the Baptist did not state that his listeners would receive power in connection with baptism with the Holy Spirit and Jesus made no such promise to anyone but the apostles. Also, Jesus did not say that the power they would receive was an integral component of baptism with the Spirit. We only know that they were to receive power in conjunction with baptism with the Spirit.

What power would they receive? It is likely the apostles did not know what to expect. Yet whatever form that power took, it was intended to assist them in their witness for Christ. Upon reflection, we now know that the powers received on the Day of Pentecost empowered the recipients to be more than mere witnesses on Christ's behalf. They were what might be considered *super-witnesses* for Christ. The powers they received on that day allowed them to persuade people, via the working of miracles, that they were speaking the truth concerning Jesus of Nazareth and the kingdom of God.

Thus, the stage was set. They were to wait in Jerusalem where, in a few days, they would be baptized with the Holy Spirit. When that occurred, the power available to them through the Holy Spirit would allow them to be the kind of witnesses Jesus required in order to establish and lead his church.

Chapter 2

The Ascension

Acts 1: 9-11

⁹And after He had said these things, He was lifted up while they were watching, and a cloud took Him up, out of their sight.

If we take into consideration the final verses of the gospel of Luke, fusing them with these introductory words in the book of Acts, it appears that either following, or in the course of, the discussion between Jesus and the apostles concerning their role as witnesses, Jesus led them to the Mount of Olives. Jesus spent much time at this location while on earth. It was a favorite place of prayer and meditation for him (Luke 21: 37).

The Mount of Olives lay just a short distance from the town of Bethany, which was within walking distance of Jerusalem. It was here that Jesus offered to his disciples the noted *Olivet Discourse* (Matthew 24), which was one of the few times Jesus gave the disciples glimpses of the future beyond his death, burial, and resurrection. Here Jesus spent his final moments on earth with the remaining apostles.

We understand from assorted passages of Scripture that when we, as men, enter heaven, we will be entering it with new spiritual bodies (1 Corinthians 15: 42-44; Philippians 3: 21; 1 John 3: 2). While we understand that Jesus' resurrection was a physical resurrection from the tomb (John 20: 27), there is much speculation about the nature of his body at the time. For instance, according to the apostle John, he refused to allow Mary Magdalene to touch him shortly after the resurrection (John 20: 15-18). Yet, the wording in that case suggests that he did not dissuade her due to concern about physical contact, but because he had something more important for her to accomplish. This view is supported even further in Matthew's record of the encounter (Matthew 28: 8-10).

Later his followers were able to have physical contact with Jesus (Luke 24: 36-39). He offered the apostle Thomas the opportunity to touch his hands and his side (John 20: 27) and he even shared meals with them (Luke 24: 40-42). Yet, while his was a physical body, he appeared before the disciples in a room with no visible means of entry. (John 20: 19). Of course, this should not be too surprising since, during his earthly life, he had walked on water (Mark 6: 45-52) and performed countless other miracles.

> [10] And as they were gazing intently into the sky while He was going, then behold, two men in white clothing stood beside them, [11] and they said, "Men of Galilee, why do you stand looking into the sky? This Jesus, who has been taken up from you into heaven, will come in the same way as you have watched Him go into heaven."

It is unknown just how long Jesus remained with the apostles at the Mount of Olives or how abrupt his ascension may have been. Perhaps he offered some words of comfort and encouragement, explaining that he must now leave them. It is possible that he simply began to rise toward the heavens as the apostles watched in horror and disbelief. He may have even spoken to them as he rose from the earth.

The apostles must have felt a sense of apprehension as Jesus rose toward the heavens and disappeared from their sight. Through the course of the last three years, they had been without him for a mere three days as he lay in the tomb. While they believed they had lost him forever at the time of his death, they were soon comforted by his resurrection. Now they watched as Jesus left them to return to heaven. He would not be with them in physical form from that day forward, and they knew it. All they could do was stare heavenward hoping to get one final glimpse of the Savior. Shading their eyes from the sun and squinting, as men are prone to do, they surely strained to avoid losing sight of him.

The apostles tarried for a while at the Mount of Olives after Jesus disappeared from sight. We are told that, as they stood there "gazing intently into the sky," two men appeared beside them. These men were dressed in white, as were those who had met the women at the tomb after Jesus' resurrection (Matthew 28: 2-4; Mark 16: 5; Luke 24: 1-4; John 20: 10-12). They were angels, messengers from God, who had been sent to nudge the apostles along as well as provide them with some encouragement, given the fact that they were now separated from their friend and teacher. The men addressed the apostles, reassuring them that this was not the last they would see of Jesus. He would return, just as he had promised while he was with them. In fact, he would eventually return in the same fashion that he had left.

A striking aspect of verse eleven is found in the phrase, "Men of Galilee," which is a pointed reference to the apostles. These men were from the region known as Galilee. The only possible exception to this was Judas Iscariot, but he was no longer with them. The apostles were chosen by Jesus in Galilee shortly after he spent time fasting in the desert and being tempted by Satan (Matthew 4: 1-22). The phrase "Men of Galilee" in complement with the balance of the narrative (vs. 6-10) depicting the exclusivity of the assembly, provides additional evidence that Jesus ascended in the presence of these eleven men.

Chapter 3

The Return to Jerusalem

Acts 1: 12-14

¹² Then they returned to Jerusalem from the mountain called Olivet, which is near Jerusalem, a Sabbath day's journey away.

The apostles were probably anxious about what to expect following Jesus' ascension. However, once they had received the words of encouragement from the angels of God, they turned back toward Jerusalem, which was a *Sabbath day's journey*[2] away.

The Pharisees, a sect of Jews who emerged as an influence in Jewish society around the second century BC, had established a number of oral rules for the Israelites that were intended to provide them with guidance in keeping the Mosaic Law. After much rabbinical debate, these rules were revised and formalized to some degree late in the second century in a work known as the Mishnah.

According to the Mosaic Law, men were to honor the Sabbath day (Exodus 20: 8). The Pharisees determined that one way men could show respect was to limit the distance they traveled on that day. Therefore, a rule was established whereby Jews were allowed to travel no more than about two-thirds of a mile on any given Sabbath. This distance was considered a Sabbath day's journey. Similarly, they reasoned that for men to honor the Sabbath appropriately, physical labor should be forbidden. For this reason, Jesus' disciples were chastised by the Pharisees when they were seen picking grain on the Sabbath (Luke 6: 1-2).

It is fair to say that most Pharisees began their journey toward developing these rules out of genuine concern over the Israelites properly honoring God. However, the Pharisaic system of obedience soon began to overshadow the Mosaic Law itself. The numerous regulations by which the Israelites were bound became an end in themselves rather than a means to an end. Limiting travel to a Sabbath

---

[2] "The Mishnah tells us that travel on the Sabbath was limited to two thousand cubits (*Sotah* 5: 3), which would be…about two-thirds of a mile." Longnecker, Richard N., The Expositor's Bible Commentary – Acts, p. 56.

day's journey and forbidding manual labor (such as picking grain) on the Sabbath were seen as successfully keeping the law without regard for a man's relationship with God. These manmade laws so dominated the Hebrew lifestyle as a substitute for faithfulness to God that Jesus often rebuked the Pharisees for what he considered a twisted view of God's relationship with men (Luke 6: 3-10). The fact that one's travels were measured in terms of a Sabbath day's journey, based on Pharisaic legalism, demonstrates how fully these rules permeated the lives of the Israelites.

It was this sort of mindset that the apostles would face as they sought to establish God's kingdom on earth in the form of the church. It is ironic, and perhaps a bit disturbing, that even their short walk back to Jerusalem from the Mount of Olives, as they considered the formidable task that lay before them, was measured in terms (a Sabbath day's journey) driven by the very forces that would oppose them as they sought to honor God.

> [3] When they had entered *the city*, they went up to the upstairs room where they were staying, that is, Peter, John, James, and Andrew, Philip and Thomas, Bartholomew and Matthew, James *the son* of Alphaeus, Simon the Zealot, and Judas *the son* of James.

One would think that the walk back to Jerusalem would have been difficult for the apostles. They had much to consider. They were told to wait for the Holy Spirit, yet they had already received the Spirit in their lives (John 20: 22), often performing miracles before men via the power of the Holy Spirit (Matthew 10: 1). Still, the Lord had told them to return to the city and wait, which they would do. But they would be waiting without Jesus, so they had reason to be sad.

However, Luke wrote in his gospel message to Theophilus that they "…returned to Jerusalem with great joy" (Luke 24: 52). They may not have understood exactly what to expect, but they knew it was from the Lord, so there was no reason to fear. Besides, they had just heard from the angels that Jesus would return. Now it was time to prepare for what lay in store.

Upon returning from the Mount of Olives, the apostles entered the upper room of the house where they had been staying. Many have speculated about the upper room. In whose house was this upper room to be found? Was this the room where Jesus had shared the Passover meal with them a few weeks earlier? Is this the place where they would be baptized with the Holy Spirit?

No absolute conclusions can be drawn concerning the room, but certain things can be ruled out. For instance, some have argued that this was a room located somewhere in the temple where the apostles gathered regularly to pray and worship God. Yet that view does not fit well with the description given here. According to Luke this was a place (*katameno*)[3] where the apostles were staying, or dwelling. It was where they ate and slept while they were in the city. They would not have resided at the temple.

An upper room such as this may have been found in the home of someone of means. Thus, the apostles were probably staying in the home of a Judean disciple who offered them lodging. Some have proposed that this particular home may have belonged to Mary, the mother of Mark (who traveled with Paul and Barnabas and later penned the gospel of Mark). It is a strong possibility, since Mary and Mark were disciples living in Jerusalem and we understand that Mary's house served as a meeting place on occasion. We know this to be true since, when Peter escaped from prison, he went directly to Mary's house. Thus, it was a place with which he was familiar where he could be confident that he would be welcome. In addition, when Peter arrived at the house, he found several of the disciples gathered there (Acts 12: 7-16).

The upper room mentioned here may have been the same place where Jesus met with the apostles for the Passover feast (Mark 14: 15; Luke 22: 12); although, the Greek word (*anogeon*)[4] used to describe the room where that feast was held differs from the word employed here. That fact does not preclude them from being the same room since multiple words in English and other languages can be used to identify the same item, but it does not confirm the proposition either.

In this verse, Luke provides us with a detailed record of those who returned to Jerusalem from the Mount of Olives. The list consists only of the names of the eleven apostles. This provides additional confirmation that it was the apostles who followed Jesus out of Jerusalem and then returned to the city after witnessing his ascension

---

[3] *2650. καταμενω* **katameno**, *kat-am-en'-o;* from *2596* and *3306;* to *stay fully*, **i.e.** *reside*:--abide. Strong, James, The New Exhaustive Concordance of the Bible-Dictionary of the Greek Testament, p. 40.

[4] *508. ανωγεον* **anogeon**, *an-ogue'-eh-on*; from *507* and *1093; above* the *ground*, i.e. (prop.) the *second floor* of a building; used for a *dome* or a *balcony* on the upper story:--upper room. Ibid, p. 13.

to heaven. When they returned, they retired to the upper room where they were staying, perhaps to spend some time in prayer and worship.

Some may wonder why, in this setting, Luke has focused so heavily on the apostles, even going so far as to identify them by name, when he had already provided those names in his previous letter to Theophilus (Luke 6: 12-16). The reason Luke sought to highlight these men at this time is found in the fact that Pentecost was as much about them as it was about Jesus or the Holy Spirit. Until this time they had always been in Jesus' shadow. The apostles needed to gain standing before the people such that the disciples would look to them as the leaders of the church and follow their directions. Thus, in the narrative leading up to the Day of Pentecost, Jesus having departed for heaven, the role of the apostles is underscored.

> **14** All these were continually devoting themselves with one mind to prayer, along with *the* women, and Mary the mother of Jesus, and with His brothers.

"All these" (the apostles listed in the previous verse) were of one mind, spiritually speaking. They had spent more than three years with Jesus, learning about the things of God. They understood the importance of prayer and worship. While they spent a considerable amount of time at the temple offering worship to God, their time spent in prayer and worship would not have been limited to the temple. They devoted *themselves* (once again, the apostles) *continually* to prayer. Wherever they were and whatever the occasion, the apostles found time for prayer.

Joining them in prayer were certain women, identified here simply as *"the* women." Why would Luke mention them so casually without fully identifying them? One reasonable answer would be that Theophilus may have known who these women were even from an inconsequential remark such as is found here. Luke had written his gospel to Theophilus. It makes sense that if these women were introduced in his first work, he would have no need to further explain them here.

As we consider the gospel Luke wrote, there were, in fact, certain women discussed (Luke 8: 1-3), and it is most reasonable to believe that these were the women Luke had in mind in his second work. These women had traveled with Jesus, ministering to him as he ministered to others. They included Mary Magdalene; a woman named Joanna whose husband managed Herod's household; a woman named

Susanna; and many others whose names were omitted. Mark, in his gospel, mentions certain women such as Salome and Mary, the mother of James and Joses, who were in Jerusalem at the time of the crucifixion and may also have been part of the group described here (Mark 15: 40). Matthew added to the list the mother of Zebedee's sons (Matthew 27: 56). It is also possible, and even likely, that Mary and Martha of Bethany, the sisters of Lazarus, were involved. They were some of Jesus' closest friends prior to his crucifixion and lived within walking distance of Jerusalem.

Also joining the apostles in devotion to prayer were Mary, the mother of Jesus, and some men who were presumably Jesus' half-brothers, the sons of Joseph and Mary. Interestingly, a few months earlier it was obvious that Jesus' half-brothers had not yet accepted his claim that he was the Messiah (John 7: 5). The events of the weeks prior to Pentecost, including the raising of Lazarus, and especially Jesus' own resurrection, must have persuaded them.

All of these remained faithful to Jesus. They committed themselves to prayer and worship with their eyes set toward the future. With the help of the Holy Spirit, Jesus had taught the apostles concerning the covenant of grace and the body of believers he wished to establish here on earth (Matthew 28: 19-20; Luke 24: 45). They now knew that Jesus' dream would soon become reality.

Chapter 4

The Selection of Matthias

Acts 1: 15-26

¹⁵ At this time Peter stood up among the brothers *and sisters* (a group of about 120 people was there together), and said, ¹⁶ "Brothers, the Scripture had to be fulfilled, which the Holy Spirit foretold by the mouth of David concerning Judas, who became a guide to those who arrested Jesus. ¹⁷ For he was counted among us and received his share in this ministry." ¹⁸ (Now this man acquired a field with the price of his wickedness, and falling headlong, he burst open in the middle and all his intestines gushed out. ¹⁹ And it became known to all the residents of Jerusalem; as a result that field was called Hakeldama in their own language, that is, Field of Blood.) ²⁰ "For it is written in the book of Psalms:

'MAY HIS RESIDENCE BE MADE DESOLATE,
AND MAY THERE BE NONE LIVING IN IT';
and,
'MAY ANOTHER TAKE HIS OFFICE.'

²¹ Therefore it is necessary that of the men who have accompanied us all the time that the Lord Jesus went in and out among us— ²² beginning with the baptism of John until the day that He was taken up from us—one of these *must* become a witness with us of His resurrection."

During the period of time just prior to Pentecost, there were a number of disciples in Jerusalem, a group totaling roughly one hundred twenty, although it is unclear whether that number included the apostles. If Luke intended to distinguish the apostles from the disciples, which seems to be the case, the total number would have been more like one hundred thirty. This would have included those mentioned previously (v. 14). While some of the one hundred twenty must have been Judeans who lived in and around Jerusalem, such as Martha and Mary, we know that others, like Mary Magdalene and Jesus' earthly family, came from Galilee and other locales around greater Israel.

Many of those who lived outside the Jerusalem area were probably present for the crucifixion and, once Jesus resurrected, stayed in Jerusalem to be with him. With Pentecost upon them, they would not return home until the festivities were over, especially knowing that something major was coming, per Jesus' words to the apostles.

"At this time" (v. 15) does not point to the previous verse when the apostles returned from the ascension. Luke wrote with a style where he often jumped from one event to another without warning (cf. vs. 4-8). It is unlikely that the host of disciples in Jerusalem were waiting for the apostles in the upper room when they returned from the Mount of Olives (v. 14), and they are not listed among those who joined the apostles in prayer. Therefore, *at this time* would be a reference to the time period between Jesus' ascension and the Day of Pentecost. Thus, at some point in time during that ten day stretch, the apostles met with the many disciples who were in Jerusalem. For a gathering of this magnitude, it would make sense for them to meet in a large room at the temple, another public building, or some outdoor setting like the Mount of Olives.

Whether Jesus had instructed them, or the apostles simply discussed the situation among themselves, we do not know. It may have been a result of Holy Spirit revelation. Such revelation may have come to the apostles when Jesus *opened their minds* so that they could understand Scripture (Luke 24: 45) Nonetheless, the apostles realized that they had a responsibility to replace Judas, restoring the number of apostles to twelve. Peter did not claim that Judas was never really a part of the ministry. On the contrary, he stated that "he was counted among us and received his share in this ministry" (v. 17). However, now that Judas was gone, it was upon the shoulders of the apostles to seek his replacement.

Judas grieved over his decision to betray Jesus, but he had not approached God to seek forgiveness. Yet, he had not committed what would be considered an unpardonable sin. As we consider New Testament teachings, there is every reason to believe that Judas could have received forgiveness for what he had done. Of course, it would have been difficult for him to take on the role of an apostle since he would have had no credibility among the people, but it is possible that, had he humbled himself and repented, he could have been forgiven by God. Nonetheless, his guilt was more than he could bear, which led to his own suicide. Hanging himself, his body fell a distance to the ground where it burst open when he landed.

Peter spoke to the disciples about Scripture being fulfilled. He explained that Judas's betrayal and demise was foreseen in the Old Testament. However, since Judas had returned the thirty pieces of silver to those from whom he had received it (Matthew 27: 3-5) this portrayal of him purchasing a field with that same money is intended to be figurative rather than literal. The chief priests and elders who received the money from Judas in turn took that money and purchased a potters field as a burial ground, an action that was foreshadowed in the Old Testament (Jeremiah 32: 6-11). Peter apparently considered the use of Judas's blood money the equivalent of Judas purchasing the piece of land.

In citing the Old Testament, Peter did not offer up a prophecy specific to Judas but quoted two separate Psalms that he evidently believed provided a proper parallel to the situation they had faced with respect to Judas (Psalm 69: 25; 109: 8). Just as king David's allies had turned against him, Judas had turned against Christ and, like David's betrayers, Judas must be replaced.

There is much speculation, but Judas's reasons for betraying Christ are not revealed in the Bible. It is unlikely that the money he received was his entire motivation. Some believe he was attempting to force Jesus' hand toward restoring Israel and moving against Rome. Still, it was the *fact* of Judas's betrayal, and not his motivation, that forced the apostles to find his replacement.

Once Judas was replaced, there would again be twelve apostles. The number twelve would serve them well. First of all, it would provide them with covenant credibility among the people. This number was critical to Israelite history, as it represented the number of the tribes of Israel. Without something to link them to the Abrahamic covenant, the apostles' task would be made more difficult. Many people would remain unconvinced who otherwise might accept Christ.

All this while, Peter was speaking to the one hundred twenty disciples who had gathered together. He wanted them to understand that Judas was to be replaced. He also wanted them to be fully aware of the apostles' approach to filling the apostolic vacancy including the qualifications necessary for a man to be eligible for the position. Those credentials are examined here and are later touched upon briefly by the apostle Paul (1 Corinthians 9: 1).

Peter explained to the disciples that for a man to become an apostle, he must have traveled with Jesus and the apostles through the entirety of Jesus' ministry. Thus, he would have been required to spend the past three years with them, learning from Jesus' own lips. Peter described the time frame as "beginning with the baptism of John until the day that He was taken up from us" (v. 22). This would have provided any candidate with the training that was necessary for the position of apostle.

The apostle Paul did not travel with Jesus and the other apostles. He was, according to his own words, "...one untimely born" (1 Corinthians 15: 8). Paul was the exception to the qualifications stated by Peter in the selection of Matthias. Nonetheless, Paul's apostleship was legitimate in that he was chosen directly by Jesus to serve as an apostle to the Gentiles (Acts 9: 15; Galatians 1: 1). He received from Jesus the training necessary for him to accomplish the ministry to which he was called (Galatians 2: 7-8).

Other men were considered apostles (Acts 14: 4, 14), but not in the same sense as Paul and the twelve. The Greek word translated *apostle*[5] literally means *one sent*. When used generically, it does not speak of the special office of *apostle* that is depicted in this case, but to messengers like Barnabas who were sent to declare the Word of God. Scripture does not indicate that Barnabas or any others were set aside for this special office. B. W. Johnson, in a discussion of the use of this word in the fourteenth chapter of the book of Acts, explained it as follows:

> The term "apostles" ... is applied in the New Testament a number of times to persons not of the twelve, but apostolic men (see 2 Cor. 8: 23). Paul was an apostle chosen by the Lord, and Barnabas was an apostolic missionary, sent out (apostle means "one sent") by the Holy Spirit.[6]

Once chosen, the newest apostle would enjoy all of the promises afforded the other apostles. This would include Jesus' promise of power when the Holy Spirit arrived (v. 8). However, he would also share in the responsibilities of an apostle, and those responsibilities were great. He would help provide witness (he, too, would be a *super-witness*) to the Israelite nation concerning Jesus Christ and God's covenant of grace.

As with Peter's use of the word *us* in identifying Judas as having a legitimate share in the apostolic ministry (v. 17), when Peter mentions *us* in these verses, it is not a reference to the one hundred twenty disciples, but a specific reference to the apostles. Many of the one

---

[5] *652. αποστολoφ* **apostolos**, *ap-os'-tol-os*; from *649*; a *delegate*; spec. an *ambassador* of the Gospel; officially a *commissioner* of Christ ["*apostle*"] (with miraculous powers):--apostle, messenger, he that is sent. Ibid, p. 15.

[6] Johnson, B. W., The People's New Testament with Explanatory Notes, pp. 478-479.

hundred twenty disciples had not traveled with Jesus during his ministry. This is an important distinction since several doctrinal disputes have surfaced beginning with this meeting between the apostles and the one hundred twenty disciples. Thus, it is important to keep before us even those details that may seem insignificant.

In saying that the candidate must have "accompanied us" (v. 21), Peter was saying that the man must have accompanied the apostles as they had accompanied Jesus. Similarly, if *us* refers to the apostles on that point, it also refers to the apostles at each other point in the narrative. For instance, when Peter mentions that Jesus "went in and out among us" (v. 21), he is referencing the apostles. The same can be said regarding "the day that He was taken up from us" (v. 22) and the role of the newest apostle as "a witness with us of His resurrection" (v. 22)

> [23] So they put forward two men, Joseph called Barsabbas (who was also called Justus), and Matthias. [24] And they prayed and said, "You, Lord, who know the hearts of all *people*, show which one of these two You have chosen [25] to occupy this ministry and apostleship from which Judas turned aside to go to his own place." [26] And they drew lots for them, and the lot fell to Matthias; and he was added to the eleven apostles.

Before addressing the selection of Judas's replacement, it is imperative that we consider an issue in these verses that provides for the early stages of considerable separation of doctrine among men. Once again, the issue surrounds the use of pronouns in the text.

The narrative states that *they* nominated two men for the role of apostle, presumably out of a group of men who met the qualifications previously noted by Peter. The word *they* occurs three times in this short segment while the word *them*, obviously referring to the two candidates, appears once. The question to be considered is: *Who, among those present at the time, does Luke have in mind with his use of the pronoun 'they'?*

A couple of possibilities have been offered in discussions surrounding this passage. Some men have concluded that the one hundred twenty disciples, along with the apostles, nominated and voted upon Judas' replacement. Others have determined that, while the one hundred twenty were in attendance, only the apostles were involved in the actual selection process. Which view is correct? In order to answer that question, we must consider in greater detail how Matthias was chosen as an apostle.

Since no new antecedents are introduced within this section of Scripture that would serve to affect the identities of those whom the author has in mind, we can conclude that whoever *they* are in verse twenty-three, the same group is also being depicted each time the word is used. Therefore, those who "put forward two men" (v. 23) also "prayed" (v. 24) and "drew lots for them" (v. 26).

The process by which a new apostle was chosen to replace Judas was not, as some men maintain, a vote of the general assembly; nor were the candidates nominated for the position based upon a consensus of the one hundred twenty disciples. Authority, at this time, had been placed in the hands of the apostles, and yet, even the apostles knew they were, to some extent, limited. Certain decisions were not under their jurisdiction. Jesus had hand-picked the original twelve apostles. Therefore, they believed this was a choice only God could make. With that in mind, they prayed that *God* would choose the newest apostle; and when they finished praying, "they drew lots for them" (v. 26).[7] In this manner, it was God rather than the apostles who chose Matthias.

The Geneva Study Bible was written in the sixteenth century on the heels of the Protestant Reformation Movement. It was the first English translation of the Bible to be interpreted directly from the original Hebrew and Greek. The notes from this work often provide insights reflecting a combination of apostolic intent and reformed theology. Of course, the two do not always harmonize, but this work often offers us a deeper understanding of the thoughts of the original authors of Scripture. Such is the case here.

> Apostles must be chosen immediately from God, and therefore after prayers, Matthias is chosen by lot, which is as it were GOD'S own voice.[8]

What was involved in the process of drawing lots? First, let us determine what it was not. We can say that it was not a vote of the brethren. The decision was left in God's hands according to the prayer that was offered. Additionally, the term *drew lots* does not depict the taking of a vote. The Greek phrase is *edokan klerous autois* which, literally translated, means *they gave lots to them*. This indicates something much different than the human voting process to which we

---

[7] cast lots (NIV); gave forth their lots (KJV); cast their lots (NKJV); gave lots for them (ASV).
[8] Lilliback, Peter A., Advisory Board Chairman, 1599 Geneva Bible Restoration Project, 1599 Geneva Bible, Tolle Lege Press, p. 1093.

have become accustomed. Richard N. Longnecker, in the Expositor's Bible Commentary, noted the following concerning the practice of *casting lots*:

> The practice was common within Israel and the ancient world generally, and is probably best illustrated by Proverbs 16:33: "The lot is cast into the lap, but its every decision is from the Lord." So by the appointment of Christ himself, the full complement of apostles was restored...[9]

Various methods for casting lots were employed throughout the Old Testament, normally by someone in authority who had the standing to seek God's guidance through this practice. For instance, the land of Canaan was divided among the tribes via the casting of lots (Numbers 26: 55). Similarly, Saul, the first king of Israel, was chosen by the casting of lots in some fashion (1 Samuel 10: 20-21). Gareth Reese offers the following perspective with respect to the casting of lots. He cites a method that is reflected in Leviticus 16: 8 that would have fit the occasion quite well:

> Another way of casting lots was to write each name on a tablet, place the tablets in an urn, and shake the urn till one came out.[10]

Who cast lots in choosing Matthias? The most reasonable answer, and surely the correct answer, is that this was done by the apostles. In fact, the casting of lots may not have involved *all* of the apostles. It is possible that the lots were cast by only one or two. Still, it would be difficult to single out individual apostles in determining who *they* were, and that does not appear to be the author's intent. However, there can be little doubt that Luke had in mind the apostles when he stated, "they drew lots for them." The apostles provided the means, before the one hundred twenty witnesses, for God to make his selection.

Only two men were presented before God to be considered for the office of apostle. We are not told how many men among the disciples may have qualified for the position, given the criteria mentioned earlier (vs. 21-22). Certain others may have qualified since many had traveled with Jesus, including the seventy whom the Lord had sent out (Luke 10: 1). Yet, something about Matthias and Barsabbas made them strong candidates.

---

[9] Longnecker, Richard N., The Expositor's Bible Commentary – Acts, p. 62.
[10] Reese, Gareth L., New Testament History – Acts, p. 32.

Of the two men who were presented, Matthias was chosen by God to fill the position vacated by Judas's betrayal. According to Luke "he was added to the eleven" (v. 26). Matthias would appear with the apostles on the Day of Pentecost, and he would share equally in the apostolic ministry. It is true that Matthias's name does not appear again in the New Testament, but the same could be said of other apostles. However, he is mentioned indirectly. After his selection, each time the twelve are referenced in the New Testament (Acts 2: 14; 6: 2), we can be sure that Matthias is among them.

Chapter 5

The Holy Spirit

Acts 2: 1-4

¹ When the day of Pentecost had come, they were all together in one place.

The festival of Pentecost, also known as the Feast of Weeks, was significant for the Israelites. Originally called the Feast of Harvest (Exodus 23: 16), it was intended as a time for the Israelites to offer the firstfruits of their labor after several weeks of harvesting the grain of the fields (Leviticus 23: 17-22). It was called Feast of Weeks because it took place fifty days (seven weeks plus one day) after the offering of the first barley sheaf during the Passover celebration. At the end of that seven-week period the harvesting of the wheat was complete, and the Israelites began their celebration. The festival acquired the name *Pentecost* (Greek for fiftieth) when, as a result of Alexander's conquest, the Greek language became well-known in Palestine.

> ¹⁵ 'You shall also count for yourselves from the day after the Sabbath, from the day when you brought in the sheaf of the wave offering; there shall be seven complete Sabbaths. ¹⁶ You shall count fifty days to the day after the seventh Sabbath; then you shall present a new grain offering to the LORD. (Leviticus 23: 15-16)

As time passed, however, the Israelites lost touch with the original purpose of the festival until it became a celebration of the receiving of the Mosaic Law. This is the reason it was celebrated by the Jews of the first century. How appropriate it is, now that the law had been fulfilled, or made complete (Matthew 5: 17-18), that on this day God would establish his new covenant with men.

When the much-anticipated Day of Pentecost arrived, we find that "they were all together in one place" (v. 1) At the outset, Luke's comment raises two rather striking questions. First of all, *Who were they*? Secondly, *Where were they*?

The second question asked here is not fully addressed by the author, making the answer difficult to determine. While the question is not irrelevant, we can say that the location is far less important than the first question raised in the verse which is, *Who were they?* Unfortunately, this question has been the source of much conflict within the religious community, often sending men scurrying in various doctrinal directions. It is the reason we have, to this point, spent much time considering the identities of those men and women mentioned in various settings in the first chapter of Acts.

In the Greek language, pronouns, *per se*, do not always exist separately. Such designations are often incorporated into the characteristics or actions related to a person or group. In this instance, we find the Greek word *esan* which, when translated into English, means *they were*. Therefore, the word *they* does not appear independently in the verse, but the verb conveys that thought.

Who do men say are represented by the pronoun *they* in this verse? Basically, two answers have surfaced over the centuries among scholars and laymen alike, each one fully confident in his understanding of the passage.

Some men have proposed that Luke has identified the twelve apostles in this verse, and some sound reasoning could lead to this conclusion. First of all, the Rule of Proximity states that an antecedent must be in close proximity to the pronoun it enlists. In fact, unless there is compelling evidence to override the basic principle, a pronoun normally represents its nearest compatible antecedent.

> The pronoun must be close enough to the word it is replacing so that your reader knows whom or what you are talking about.[11]

This rule is just as important in the Greek language as it is in the English language. Applying this rule of grammar to the text before us, we need not journey far to discover a fitting antecedent. A mere eight words earlier, it appears as the final word in the previous verse. It is the word *apostles*. Because of the break that has been inserted between the first and second chapters of Acts, this connection is often lost to men who are attempting to identify who *they* are. Below is a rendition of the final verse of chapter one and the first verse of chapter two, presented as Luke originally penned the letter.

> And they drew lots for them, and the lot fell to Matthias; and he was added to the eleven apostles. When the day of Pentecost had come, they were all together in one place. (Acts 1: 26 – 2: 1)

---

[11] The Rule of Proximity, Englishplus.com.

It is easy to see why, as we consider Luke's words, some would regard the apostles as the antecedent for those who "were all together in one place" (v. 1). Strengthening this position is the fact that, in the final four verses of the previous chapter, each time the word *they* occurs, it is clearly used to identify the apostles. "They put forward two men" (v. 23). "They prayed" (v. 24). "They drew lots" (v. 26). Additionally, something that generally remains unnoticed is the fact that, to this point in the text, the one hundred twenty disciples in the previous chapter are not treated as an antecedent for any pronoun anywhere in the narrative, which makes such an interpretation here difficult.

Given this consistency and the fact that no new antecedent is introduced in the narrative to dissuade us, we have every grammatical reason to believe it was the apostles who were *together in one place*. Following is a presentation of all five verses as Theophilus would have read them:

> So they put forward two men, Joseph called Barsabbas (who was also called Justus), and Matthias. And they prayed and said, "You, Lord, who know the hearts of all *people*, show which one of these two You have chosen to occupy this ministry and apostleship from which Judas turned aside to go to his own place." And they drew lots for them, and the lot fell to Matthias; and he was added to the eleven apostles. When the day of Pentecost had come, they were all together in one place. (Acts 1: 23 – 2: 1)

Beyond the simple grammar that is involved in our search for an answer, another factor should be given serious consideration. It is a fact that, for the most part, the apostles were Luke's focus from the beginning of the letter. While Luke and Theophilus are mentioned in the introduction, they existed outside the framework of the events of the first chapter. That is to say, they were observers rather than participants. Even Jesus did not garner the attention in the first chapter that the apostles received. The angels, the women, Jesus' earthly family, and the one hundred twenty disciples, were ancillary characters by whom the apostles were surrounded. Therefore, it is difficult to dismiss the notion that Luke had the apostles in mind throughout this short narrative, including his remarks concerning those who were gathered together on the Day of Pentecost.

Those men who wrote the notes for the Geneva Study Bible drew from Luke's remarks that those gathered together were, indeed, the twelve apostles.

> The apostles being gathered together on a most solemn feast day in one place, that it might evidently appear to all the world, that they had all one office, one Spirit, one faith, are by a double sign from heaven authorized, and anointed with all the most excellent gifts of the holy Ghost and especially with an extraordinary and necessary gift of tongues…The Twelve Apostles, which were to be the Patriarchs as it were of the Church.[12]

The second group that many people claim may have been gathered together on the Day of Pentecost is all of those disciples who were present when Matthias was chosen as Judas's successor. This would have included the apostles along with the approximately one hundred twenty disciples. Many believe this is a strong possibility, and perhaps even a probability (some are fully convinced), based on Luke's comment that *they were all together in one place.* While this is the weaker grammatical argument, since the antecedent for this explanation is so far removed from the pronoun (it appears in verse fifteen of the first chapter), the proposition should still be given fair and objective consideration if we wish to honor God's Word.

Luke wrote that *they were all together.* This terminology does seem to hint that he may have had in mind a grouping different from those mentioned in the previous verses. As we consider the narrative, we are faced with two options. First, Luke may have considered that by adding Matthias to the eleven, a new and larger group had formed. Thus, *they* (the eleven plus Matthias) *were all together in one place.* The other possibility is that Luke intended to include the entire assembly of believers, thus altering the focus that had, to that point, been on the apostles.

In the previous verses, Peter and the other apostles took the steps necessary to select a new apostle. Even though the focus was on the apostles, as honest students of the Bible we recognize that all one hundred twenty disciples were *present* during the entire ceremony. At least, to this author's knowledge, no one has argued to the contrary. This means they would have been with the apostles even during the final four verses of the previous chapter, as Matthias was chosen. Everything that occurred beginning with the fifteenth verse of the previous chapter happened in their presence. They may have been silent witnesses to the selection of Matthias, but Luke's words indicate that they were in attendance at the time. Consequently, since the one

---

[12] Lilliback, Peter A., Advisory Board Chairman, 1599 Geneva Bible Restoration Project, <u>1599 Geneva Bible, Tolle Lege Press</u>, p. 1093.

hundred twenty were included, albeit as a backdrop, in the previous verse, the argument that they also might have been among those present on the Day of Pentecost cannot be casually dismissed.

It is easy to see why perceptions differ so dramatically with respect to this verse and why some believe only the apostles were gathered together while others insist that it was the larger number of believers. Both scenarios seem to fit. Therefore, based on this verse alone, it is not possible to determine conclusively which group was *all together in one place*. However, as the events of the day unfold, we will discover that Luke provides sufficient evidence for us to fully resolve this mystery.

The second question raised from Luke's remarks as he introduced the arrival of the Day of Pentecost (v. 1) is: *Where were they?* All the author has revealed in the narrative is that *they were all together in one place*. Again, a number of thoughts have been proposed. It is a simple step to determine that the setting is the city of Jerusalem. The apostles were told to wait in Jerusalem where they would receive "what the Father had promised" (v. 4). Additionally, the feast known as Pentecost was celebrated in Jerusalem. Therefore, we can conclude that these events took place there. However, it is a formidable task to determine where they met within the city.

What one believes about *who* they were will have some influence upon what one believes about *where* they were. For instance, if Luke intended to portray only the apostles as those who were gathered together, nearly any room in any house in Jerusalem would suffice. In fact, if only the apostles were involved, the upper room where they had been staying would have been well-suited to the occasion. All they needed was enough room for twelve men. However, earlier in the text the author gave specific attention to the upper room (Acts 1: 13). It seems a bit odd that a few paragraphs later he would refer to that same room simply as a *place* rather than openly identifying it. This does not disqualify the upper room as a possibility, but it does seem to diminish the likelihood that they were gathered there.

For those who believe that Luke had in mind all of the believers who were assembled together for the induction of Matthias, the upper room that housed the apostles would probably be inadequate. It is unlikely that this many disciples were gathered in a single room in any house in Jerusalem. Such a room would need to be massive, large enough to hold at least one hundred twenty people. This would have been very uncommon for a residence in Jerusalem. Therefore, it has been suggested that, rather than assembling in the upper room or an individual's house somewhere in the city, they could have gathered in a large room somewhere in the temple complex. This is a possibility given the fact that Luke had concluded his gospel to Theophilus with the observation that the apostles "…were continually in the temple praising God" (Luke 24: 53). This has been taken by J. W. McGarvey to mean, perhaps justifiably, that when the temple was open and available, the apostles were there much of the time. McGarvey concluded:

> The house in which the apostles were sitting when the Spirit came upon them was not the upper chamber in which they were abiding, but some apartment of the temple; for, as we learn from Luke's former treatise, the apostles during these days of waiting were "continually in the temple praising God;" that is, continually there through the hours in which the temple was open.[13]

Whether Luke had in mind the entire company of disciples or only the apostles, it would not be surprising to find them worshipping God in the temple at any given time. Yet, as with the ambiguities we have faced in dealing with the identity of those who were gathered together, in this segment the author is still rather stingy with clues that could lead us to discern their location. Therefore, no absolute determination can yet be made. We can only forge ahead to see what additional information might be made available to us in the coming verses.

> [2] And suddenly a noise like a violent rushing wind came from heaven, and it filled the whole house where they were sitting. [3] And tongues *that looked* like fire appeared to them, distributing themselves, and *a tongue* rested on each one of them. [4] And they were all filled with the Holy Spirit and began to speak with different tongues, as the Spirit was giving them *the ability* to speak out. (Acts 2: 2-4)

As they joined together (whether the apostles only or the ensemble of disciples), it is likely they were worshipping God. This would explain why they were all together. In fact, it is probable that when a few of them gathered together, the result was some form of worship or godly fellowship. The days between Jesus' ascension and the Day of Pentecost were filled with prayer and fellowship for the apostles and those around them (Acts 1: 14). The intensity of worship and single-

---

[13] McGarvey, J. W., New Commentary on Acts, pp 21-22.

mindedness they shared must have helped lift each one's faith to the level necessary for them to accomplish the goals God had established.

While few may realize the fact, it is interesting to note that in the Hebrew language, the word interpreted as *spirit* and the word interpreted as *wind* are one and the same. In fact, this same word, which is *ruwach*,[14] is also often translated as *breath*. The same is true with respect to the Greek language where *pneuma*,[15] the word for *spirit*, is also translated *breath* or *wind*.

The relationship between wind and spirit could be a contributing factor leading to the noise that accompanied the Holy Spirit's arrival. It is difficult to say if the sound of wind naturally accompanied the Spirit or if the noise was unique to this occasion. Other times when the Holy Spirit arrived among men, no noise was reported (Acts 10: 44; 19: 6). That does not mean such a noise did not accompany the Spirit on those occasions, but none is mentioned. In fact, there may have been no actual wind as part of the equation here. Luke notes the *sound* of heavy wind but does not say that the wind itself actually materialized. Then again, this incident was unique in other ways, too.

The house where they were assembled was filled. Filled with what? Surely the house was filled with the noise that accompanied the Holy Spirit. Luke stated, "suddenly a noise like a violent rushing wind came from heaven, and it filled the whole house" (v. 2). It is likely the noise was deafening, resembling the roar of a tornado. The Holy Spirit made no small entrance, especially on this most momentous occasion. It is also reasonable to believe that, just as the noise filled the house, the Spirit filled the house. Thus, those present would have been immersed (baptized) in the Spirit.

---

[14] *7307*. **uhuwr ruwach**, *roo'-akh*; from *7306*; *wind*; by resemblance *breath*, i.e. a sensible (or even violent) exhalation; fig. *life, anger, unsubstantiality*; by extens. *a region* of the sky; by resemblance spirit, but only of a rational being (includ. its expression and functions):--air, anger, blast, breath, X cool, courage, mind, X quarter, X side, spirit ([-ual]), tempest, X vain, ([whirl-]) wind **(-y)**. Strong, James, The New Exhaustive Concordance of the Bible-Dictionary of the Hebrew Bible, p. 107.

[15] *4151*. πνευμα **pneuma**, *pnyoo'-mah*; from {A.} *4154*; a current of air, i.e. *breath* (blast) or a *breeze*; by anal. or fig. a *spirit*, i.e. (human) the rational soul, (by impl.) *vital principle*, mental *disposition*, etc., or (superhuman) an angel, daemon, or (divine) God, Christ's spirit, the Holy Spirit:--ghost, life, spirit (-ual, -ually), mind. Comp. {B.} *5590*. Strong, James, The New Exhaustive Concordance of the Bible-Dictionary of the Greek Testament, p. 58.

Luke describes for us "tongues *that looked like* fire" (v. 3) that accompanied the thunderous noise that filled the house. Just as the *sound* of wind did not necessarily manifest itself in an actual violent wind, these tongues are not described as *actual* tongues of fire, but they did resemble fire. That is to say, when they came in contact with physical objects, those objects did not burn up as they would have with fire, just as the fiery bush was not consumed in Moses's presence (Exodus 3: 2). We know this because these tongues *rested on* each one who was in the house at the time, yet no harm came to anyone.

They were surrounded by an incredibly loud noise with what appeared to be a flame resting upon each one present. It must have been an inspiring, almost indescribable feeling as they realized something magnificent was happening. Surely this was the moment for which they had been waiting. Now they would receive "what the Father had promised" (Acts 1: 4). It must be, then, that the Holy Spirit would soon be upon them.

The Holy Spirit had interacted intimately with men over the centuries. The Old Testament speaks of a man by the name of Bezalel being filled "...with the Spirit of God" (Exodus 31: 3; 35: 31). The Spirit also often spoke through the prophets (cf. 2 Samuel 23: 2; Nehemiah 9: 20; Isaiah 48: 16; Ezekiel 2: 2) and *came upon* men at various times (cf. Judges 3: 10; 11: 29; 2 Chronicles 15: 1). Additionally, King David prayed that God would not "...take your Holy Spirit from me" (Psalm 51: 11). Luke noted that Zacharias, father to John the Baptist, was "...filled with the Holy Spirit" (Luke 1: 67) and that John the Baptist was "...filled with the Holy Spirit while still in his mother's womb" (Luke 1: 15). How those experiences compared with Pentecost we do not know, but we do know that this day was special.

In an historic biblical moment, "they were all filled with the Holy Spirit" (v. 4). It was a most miraculous event as the Spirit whelmed their very being, apparently on both a physical and spiritual plane. In essence, they became one with God as he shared the Holy Spirit with them in a breathtaking fashion.

Seemingly without warning, each one present began to speak in what the author describes as *other tongues*.[16] That is to say, they spoke not of their own volition, but in tongues, or languages, provided to

---

[16] Other languages (NRSV)

them by the Holy Spirit. They were speaking in ways well beyond their individual abilities. The Holy Spirit came upon them and they spoke miraculously "as the Spirit was giving them *the ability* to speak out" (v. 4).

Note that Luke did not say that they spoke in *unknown* tongues, but in *other*[17] tongues.[18] This is a critical distinction with respect to what these believers experienced on that day. They did not babble with incomprehensible sounds that no one could understand. We discover in the coming narrative that other men and women recognized the languages they were speaking as well as the message that was shared through those languages.

In this section, standing out like the proverbial sore thumb is the word *house* (v. 2). Perhaps this word can help us narrow the field concerning those who gathered together on the Day of Pentecost, as well as where they gathered together. The word Luke used that has been interpreted into English as *house* is the Greek word *oikos*.[19] As can be seen from Strong's characterization of this word (see footnote), it could be used as a designation for either a house or a temple. However, generally speaking, the word refers to a house or home. Also, in essentially every English translation of the Bible the word has been interpreted to mean *house* in this setting,[20] presumably because that is the commonly accepted meaning. Obscuring the picture slightly is the fact that there is one instance in the New Testament when the author apparently used this word to reference the temple.

> ...from the blood of Abel to the blood of Zechariah, who was killed between the altar and the *house of God*; yes, I tell you, it shall be charged against this generation.' (Luke 11: 51) – emphasis added

---

[17] *2087 ετεροω* **heteros**, *het'-er-os*; of uncert. affin.; (an-, the) *other or different*:-- altered, else, next (day), one, (an-) other, some, strange. Strong, James, The New Exhaustive Concordance of the Bible-Dictionary of the Greek Testament, p. 33.
[18] *1100 γλωσσα.* **glossa**, *gloce'-sah*; of uncert. affin.; the *tongue*; by impl. a *language* (spec. one naturally unacquired):--tongue. Ibid, p. 20.
[19] *3624. οικοω* **oikos**, *oy'-kos*; of uncert. affin.; a *dwelling* (more or less extensive, lit. or fig.); by impl. a *family* (more or less related, lit. or fig.):--home, house (-hold), temple. Ibid, p. 51.
[20] In the English paraphrased translation entitled *The Message*, *oikos* is translated as *building* in this context.

This word *oikos*, which is translated *house* in virtually all biblical settings, is rendered *house* of God[21] in this verse from the gospel of Luke. What makes this even more curious is that Luke, who penned the gospel, is the same author who wrote about the noise that "filled the whole house" (v. 2). Could he again have the temple in mind?

Without exception, in every other instance where Luke wrote about the temple, he used either *heiron*[22] or *naos*[23] to identify the temple. In fact, these words appear more than forty times in Luke's writings. Additionally, in the single setting where we know Luke used *oikos* to point to the temple, a strong argument can be made that his intent was to portray it as *God's house*, or *residence*. This is the understanding of many interpreters. On the other hand, between his two letters to Theophilus, Luke used the word *oikos* (or a derivative) nearly one hundred times. With the one exception given above (Luke 11: 51), the word was always used to identify a house, home, or family (e.g., the house of David).

When determining the meaning of a word that has been translated from another language, unless there is compelling evidence to the contrary, it is wise to accept that the word is intended to represent its *most common meaning*. This is especially true when that meaning is overwhelmingly recognized as the most accepted and is employed as such repeatedly by the author, as in this case. When someone said *oikos*, those listening would have instantly pictured a house, not the temple. Similarly, when Luke mentioned *oikos*, he was discussing a house or home. That is why virtually all English translators have agreed upon the meaning of *house* in this setting.

What does this tell us about the place where the Holy Spirit came upon the assembly? It does not reveal a lot about the exact location, but it lessens the likelihood that they were in the temple at the time and makes it more likely that they were at a private home – perhaps even the *upper room*. It is this author's opinion that, in his wisdom, God wanted Luke to be a bit ambiguous here, knowing the shrine and

---

[21] Sanctuary (ASV; NIV); temple (KJV; NKJV).
[22] *2411.* ιερον **hieron**, *hee-er-on'*; neut. of {A.} *2413*; a *sacred* place, i.e. the entire precincts (whereas {B.} *3485* denotes the central sanctuary itself) of the *Temple* (at Jerus. or elsewhere):--temple. Strong, James, The New Exhaustive Concordance of the Bible-Dictionary of the Greek Testament, p. 37.
[23] *3485.* ναοω, **naos**, *nah-os'*; from a *prim.* ναιω **naio** (to *dwell*); a *fane, shrine, temple*:--shrine, temple. Comp. *2411*. Ibid, p. 49.

ensuing idol worship that men almost certainly would have developed were the exact location known. There is a strong likelihood that this is the reason God kept Moses's burial place a secret from men (Deuteronomy 34: 6), and we can reasonably infer this in the case of the location where the Spirit was poured out on the Day of Pentecost.

What can we learn from this revelation concerning the identity of those in the house? The high probability that those who received the Holy Spirit were in a private home only reinforces the position that it was the apostles who were *all together in one place*. It is true that this does not prove that the apostles were alone, but it certainly provides additional support for that view.

In these three short verses (vs. 2-4) we are met with a number of pronouns that could be given consideration. For instance, the word *they* appears three times in this segment. Similarly, the pronoun *them* occurs three times. Yet nothing about these words adds to or detracts substantially from either side of the argument over those who were gathered together, received the Holy Spirit, and spoke in other tongues. Therefore, their identity remains veiled for the moment.

Chapter 6

The Crowd

Acts 2: 5-13

⁵ Now there were Jews residing in Jerusalem, devout men from every nation under heaven. ⁶ And when this sound occurred, the crowd came together and they were bewildered, because each one of them was hearing them speak in his own language. ⁷ They were amazed and astonished, saying, "Why, are not all these who are speaking Galileans?

Starting with their exile in Babylonia (circa 600 BC), the Israelites had been dominated by a few foreign nations. Following their capture by Nebuchadnezzar they were subject to the Persians, the Greeks, and now Rome. It is not surprising, then, that many of the Jews who lived in Jerusalem in the mid first century had returned there from various locations in Asia, Africa, and Europe. When the opportunity presented itself, they had chosen their fatherland, and its chief city, as their home.

The narrative suggests that those who filled the streets of Jerusalem on that day were Jews who resided in the city. Some men make a point of this based on the word *katoikeo,*[24] translated *residing* (v. 5), which leaves that impression. However, in the next section we will find some clarification concerning Luke's thoughts. Apparently, there were those among them, like the apostles, who were visitors to the city (v. 10). Therefore, it appears that Luke was not attempting to limit the crowd to Jerusalem residents, but that he intended to include those who had returned to the city and were *staying* in anticipation of Pentecost. For many it would have been an extended stay that took in both the Passover and Pentecost.

On this, the Day of Pentecost, the streets of Jerusalem would have been bustling with activity as the residents engaged in the preparation for such an important festival. With the verbal chatter and numerous other sounds surrounding them, imagine how startled they must have

---

[24] *2730 κατοικεω* **katoikeo,** *kat-oy-keh'-o; from 2596 and 3611;* to *house permanently,* i.e. *reside* (lit. or fig.):--dwell (-er), inhabitant (-ter). Ibid, p. 41.

been to have a thunderous noise fill the air, drowning out everything else. Since no wind is mentioned in the text, the fact that they heard the kind of sounds that could only come from a powerful wind must have been perplexing. By the thousands they began moving in the direction of the commotion.

When they arrived at the source of the disturbance, they came upon certain people who were speaking a multitude of languages all at the same time. As if this alone was not enough to confound them, they became even more confused when they discovered who was speaking. What was most astonishing was that the speakers were all Galileans. Why would they be so surprised that Galileans were speaking in these various languages? According to Richard N. Longnecker:

> Galileans had difficulty pronouncing gutturals and had the habit of swallowing syllables when speaking, so they were looked down upon by the people of Jerusalem as being provincial (cf. Mark 14: 70).[25]

In that same vein, Gareth L. Reese notes concerning the people of Galilee:

> Galilean men came from a despised district (John 7: 52) where education was scanty, the standard low, and the spoken dialect was peculiar... The Galilean accent was easily recognized even though the apostles were speaking languages other than Greek or Aramaic, for Galileans had difficulty with certain guttural sounds (similar to the Japanese who have trouble with the "L" in English). In addition, the apostles' dress would have aided in their identification...[26]

These characteristics that were so obviously attributable to Galileans may have been partly responsible for giving Peter away on the day of the crucifixion. At that time, some men insisted that he was one of Jesus' followers, an accusation he vehemently denied (Mark 14: 66-72).

On the Day of Pentecost these distinctive Galilean attributes may not have been particularly noticeable to the crowd as these Galileans spoke in various languages (*glossa*[27] – v. 4). The narrative denotes that everyone heard them speak not only in different languages, but also in

---

[25] Longnecker, Richard N., The Expositor's Bible Commentary – Acts, p. 68.
[26] Reese, Gareth L., New Testament History – Acts, p. 50.
[27] *1100.* glwssa **glossa**, *gloce'-sah*; of uncert. affin.; the *tongue*; by impl. a *language* (spec. one naturally unacquired):--tongue. Strong, James, The New Exhaustive Concordance of the Bible-Dictionary of the Greek Testament, p. 20.

different dialects (*dialektos*[28] - v. 6). However, many in Jerusalem may have recognized them as Galileans from conversations in the temple, etc., over the course of the past few weeks and would have been astounded by the fact that these men were speaking other dialects so fluently.

The people of Galilee were not considered social or political elites. On the contrary, they were viewed with a measure of indignation by many of the privileged and influential in Judea. That a group of Galileans would be discovered at the center of an event of seemingly epic proportions was difficult for the Jews in Jerusalem to take in. While the circumstance itself was beyond belief, the fact that it involved Galileans explains Luke's observance that they were "amazed and astonished" (v. 7), as though he was attempting to describe something to Theophilus that was beyond description.

Whereas the tongues themselves were an incredible phenomenon, there exists another major point of interest in this portion of Luke's narrative. As we consider who, among the believers, were "all together in one place" (v. 2: 1), the Jews in Jerusalem have offered a significant piece of evidence. First of all, we were told by Luke that all of the believers who were gathered together on that day received the Holy Spirit and began to speak in other languages (vs. 3-4). We now know that those who were gathered together, received the Holy Spirit, and spoke in tongues were all Galileans.

As with the angels who appeared at the Mount of Olives and proclaimed, "Men of Galilee" (1: 11) in reference to the apostles, so these Jews of Jerusalem recognized those who were speaking in various languages as Galileans. Surely, then, it was the apostles who were *together in one place*. Yet, some may question this conclusion. After all, they may say, is it not possible that *all* of the disciples were Galileans?

We can conclude from God's Word that the apostles were, indeed, from the region known as Galilee (we can assume this is true of Matthias also since we can be confident that he was with the apostles). Additionally, we can deduce that certain other disciples were Galileans including Mary Magdalene, Jesus' family, and probably several others, since some women had followed Jesus from Galilee (Matthew 27: 55).

---

[28] *1258*. dialektoj **dialektos**, *dee-al'-ek-tos*; from *1256*; a (mode of) *discourse*, i.e. "*dialect*":--language, tongue. Ibid, p. 22.

However, it is not only highly unlikely that all of the one hundred twenty disciples were from Galilee, but the proposition is unrealistic given the diversity of Jesus' followers.

Many of Jesus' disciples were from Galilee, but many were not. Mary, Martha, and Lazarus, whom Jesus had raised from the dead just prior to his own death, hailed from Bethany, which was well within walking distance of Jerusalem. It is difficult to imagine a gathering of disciples that did not include them since they were among Jesus' closest friends. We can say with certainty that it would have been difficult to keep Mary from this kind of fellowship (cf. Luke 10: 38-42). Similarly, a man named Joseph who was from Arimathaea, a stretch of land located in the region known as Ephraim between Jericho and Joppa, had given his tomb as Jesus' burial place (Matthew 27: 57). Since he had purchased a tomb in the area, it is likely he lived in Jerusalem. Therefore, as with Mary, Martha, and Lazarus, it is probable that he was among the one hundred twenty disciples. However, he was not Galilean.

Zaccheus and Bartimaeus both came from Jericho on the eastern border of Judea, although it is difficult to know if they might have been in Jerusalem at the time. They were, however, representative of the diversity of Jesus' disciples throughout the region. Christ had followers stretching from Tyre in the north (Mark 7) to Capernaum in Galilee (John 4) to Sychar in Samaria (John 4) to the cities of Jericho (Luke 18-19), Bethany (John 11-12), and Jerusalem (Matthew 26) in Judea. Only a portion of Jesus' disciples were from the region known as Galilee.

One convincing piece of evidence concerning the makeup of the one hundred twenty disciples is the fact that John Mark, who authored the gospel of Mark, and his mother Mary (both were mentioned earlier), were residents of Jerusalem. They were not Galileans, yet they were among Jesus' early disciples. Scholars generally agree that these two were among the one hundred twenty disciples mentioned in the first chapter of Acts. Some also assume that the upper room that housed the apostles (Acts 1: 13) was located at Mary's home and that this was where Jesus celebrated the Passover with the disciples (Mark 14: 12-26) prior to his death. J. W. McGarvey remarks concerning John Mark:

Thus it appears that from the very beginning of the Church, if not during the life of Jesus, John Mark enjoyed the company of the apostles in his home...[29]

If the house where the apostles were staying was not Mary's house, it is a reasonable assumption that it was the home of another believer living in Jerusalem who had made his/her house available to them. Longnecker comments:

> On their return to Jerusalem, the disciples "went upstairs to the room where they were staying." The use of the definitive article in speaking of "the room" (*to hyperoon*) and the emphatic place these words have at the beginning of the clause suggest that the room was well known to the early Christians—perhaps the room where Jesus and his disciples kept the Passover just before his crucifixion (Mark 14: 12-16). Perhaps it was the room where he appeared to some of them after he rose from the dead (Luke 24: 33-43; cf. John 20: 19, 26). Or, though this is more inferential, it may have been a room in the house of John Mark's mother, where the church later met (Acts 12: 12).[30]

This is a lot of data to take in, but it is critical if we are to correctly interpret the events of Pentecost. What can we conclude from such a barrage of information about Jesus' followers? We can say with confidence that not every disciple in Jerusalem prior to the Day of Pentecost was a Galilean transplant. We can also establish, based on this knowledge, that not all of the one hundred twenty disciples were *together in one place* when the Day of Pentecost arrived.

Some may question this conclusion, arguing that perhaps the apostles along with only those disciples who were Galileans received the Holy Spirit and spoke in tongues on that day. The difficulty with this line of reasoning is that the text does not allow for it. When Luke stated that "they were all together in one place" (v. 1), he limited the possibilities. He was either referring to the apostles as a whole or he was pointing to the entire complement of disciples in the company of the apostles. The verse simply does not offer the option that *all* of the apostles and *some* of the disciples were gathered together. Luke has yet to tell us *why* the experience was limited to the apostles, but we can be confident that, according to Scripture, only the apostles spoke in tongues on that day.

---

[29] McGarvey, J. W., New Commentary on Acts, p. 258.
[30] Longnecker, Richard N., The Expositor's Bible Commentary – Acts, p. 56.

⁸ And how *is it that* we each hear *them* in our own language to which we were born? ⁹ Parthians, Medes, and Elamites, and residents of Mesopotamia, Judea, and Cappadocia, Pontus and Asia, ¹⁰ Phrygia and Pamphylia, Egypt and the parts of Libya around Cyrene, and visitors from Rome, both Jews and proselytes, ¹¹ Cretans and Arabs—we hear them speaking in our *own* tongues of the mighty deeds of God."

Evidently the apostles moved into the street as they continued to speak in a variety of languages. It would have been difficult to fit the thousands who thronged to them in a single building. Even in the temple court it would have been crowded. As the multitude encircled the apostles, it makes sense that those of the one hundred twenty disciples (Acts 1: 15) who remained in Jerusalem for Pentecost would have been drawn to the same noise and were present at the time.

Many in the crowd were puzzled. How could these Galileans speak in different languages and how could each man hear in his own language? Most of the Jews who witnessed the event would have been fluent in Aramaic and/or Hebrew, which were prominent in the region, but they also spoke the languages where they were born and raised. In all, depending on how they are counted, it appears that roughly fifteen languages were represented by those in attendance (some maintain that the districts of Libya may have involved more than one language).

The fact that at least fifteen languages were represented by those in the crowd, with only twelve apostles to speak them, adds an additional element to the miracle of Pentecost. After all, if people in the crowd who spoke these many languages could each hear in his own native tongue, it suggests that the miracle was multi-dimensional. Either the apostles were speaking multiple languages simultaneously or the miracle was not merely on the tongues of the apostles, but on the ears of their audience. Since the Spirit had come upon the apostles alone in order to manifest this miracle, it is likely that it was restricted to the tongues of the apostles. This was the view of the translators of the Geneva Study Bible.

> Not that they spake with one voice, and many languages were heard, but that the Apostles spake with strange tongues; for else the miracle had rather been in the hearers, whereas now it is in the speakers…[31]

---

[31] Lilliback, Peter A., Advisory Board Chairman, 1599 Geneva Bible Restoration Project, <u>1599 Geneva Bible, Tolle Lege Press</u>, p. 1094.

Not only was the miracle of tongues breathtaking for those who were present, but the message the apostles spoke was illuminating. The people recognized that the apostles, in these many languages, were proclaiming "the mighty deeds of God" (v. 11). The presence of the miracle of tongues would have given credence to that message, which was unquestionably God's intent.

> [12] And they all continued in amazement and great perplexity, saying to one another, "What does this mean?" [13] But others were jeering and saying, "They are full of sweet wine!"

The confusion must have been contagious as people in the crowd began whispering among themselves. Here were twelve Galileans speaking multiple languages while proclaiming the message of God. Although Jesus and the apostles had performed many miracles over the past few years, it had been a while since the Jews experienced something of this magnitude. They had read of the plagues in Egypt (Exodus 7-12), the crossing of the Red Sea (Exodus 13: 17-14: 29), the walls of Jericho (Joshua 6), and numerous other miraculous events described in the Old Testament that their forefathers experienced. That, however, was ancient history. Centuries had passed since Israelites had witnessed something so extraordinary. Therefore, it is not surprising that it was difficult for these men and women to comprehend what was happening. Miracles like this were not especially common in first century Jerusalem.

The stories of numerous healings, casting out demons, and Lazarus rising from the dead, must have circulated throughout the region. Still, most of the crowd on this day had never witnessed something so spectacular. Some may have heard about or even participated in the feeding of the five thousand (Matthew 14: 13-21), but that was a rather subtle miracle in comparison to the splendor of Pentecost. It is no wonder they would ask, "What does this mean?" (v. 12).

As is true of any large gathering, this crowd held some skeptics. They may have believed this was some kind of a magic trick or prank but could not see how the apostles would be so convincing as to pull off such a hoax. While claiming that the apostles might be drunk with wine may seem like a ridiculous proposition to us, given the circumstances, it was probably all these doubters had to offer, and offer it they did. They sought to mock the apostles and make them appear foolish before the throngs of people. However, it was the mockers who would be made to look like fools. It would not take long for many to realize that what they were witnessing was a grand miracle in the likeness of those seen by their ancestors in days past.

Chapter 7

The Fulfillment of Prophecy

Acts 2: 14-21

¹⁴ But Peter, taking his stand with the *other* eleven, raised his voice and declared to them: "Men of Judea and all you who live in Jerusalem, know this, and pay attention to my words. ¹⁵ For these people are not drunk, as you assume, since it is *only* the third hour of the day;

Peter had, for some time, taken the lead among the apostles. He was, after all, in Jesus' inner circle, which also included James and John. He may have taken the lead partly because he was usually the first to speak in any given situation, but he clearly had a special relationship with Christ and was respected by the others. Therefore, on an occasion like this it is not surprising to find that it was Peter who addressed the crowd. Additionally, it was Peter to whom Jesus had given the keys to the kingdom (Matthew 16: 19), placing him in a conspicuous position to open doors, like the one he faced now.

The charge of drunkenness sparked a response from the apostles. Peter, moving to address the accusation and help settle the crowd, stood up with the other eleven apostles to answer such an outrageous allegation. His answer was not the kind that would be given by someone who was under heavy influence from wine. Instead, he was articulate and rational in his response.

The suggestion of drunkenness, if left unanswered, would hinder the message the apostles wished to share. Therefore, it was imperative that they resolve the matter quickly. Presenting the other eleven apostles to the crowd and speaking on their behalf (as well as his own), Peter made it clear that they were not drunk as some had suggested. His answer seemed to go out to the assembly in general rather than to a few cynics, so it is possible that the assertion of drunkenness had begun to gather some steam as it spread through the gathering.

Peter went on to point out what a ridiculous notion this was since it was only 9:00 o'clock in the morning. The third hour of the day was the morning hour of prayer. No self-respecting Jew who kept the hour of prayer would even consider taking wine at this time in the morning. Peter's answer did not completely refute the charge, since it is possible to drink wine in the morning, but the argument concerning the hour of prayer would have been taken seriously by those in the crowd. Luke had described them as "devout men from every nation under heaven" (v. 5). They were faithful Jews (that is, faithful to the Mosaic Law) who had not yet heard the message of Jesus Christ. (One might add that inebriation is not generally known to cause a person to spontaneously break out in multiple foreign languages, making the accusation itself a bit foolish).

While the evidence is no longer needed, since the issue has already been put to rest, we find additional support here for the Spirit falling only upon the apostles on the Day of Pentecost. When Peter addressed the charge of drunkenness from members of the crowd, he was defending the apostles. It was against them that the accusation had been made. Peter stood "with the *other* eleven" (v. 14) as they faced the crowd together and proclaimed to the crowd, "these people are not drunk" (v. 15), including himself in the mix. Thus, he was not speaking of the one hundred twenty disciples, but of the apostles. Although the Greek *houtoi*, translated "these people"[32] is masculine, it is often translated without respect to gender. In this case, the apostles (v. 1) serve as the antecedent, making the designation sure. For this reason, certain translators have rendered the meaning "these men" (ISV, RSV). Having made his point, Peter continued:

> [16] but this is what has been spoken through the prophet Joel:
>
> [17] 'AND IT SHALL BE IN THE LAST DAYS,' God says,
> 'THAT I WILL POUR OUT MY SPIRIT ON ALL MANKIND;
> AND YOUR SONS AND YOUR DAUGHTERS WILL PROPHESY,
> AND YOUR YOUNG MEN WILL SEE VISIONS,
> AND YOUR OLD MEN WILL HAVE DREAMS;
> [18] AND EVEN ON MY MALE AND FEMALE SERVANTS
> I WILL POUR OUT MY SPIRIT IN THOSE DAYS,
> And they will prophesy.
> [19] AND I WILL DISPLAY WONDERS IN THE SKY ABOVE
> AND SIGNS ON THE EARTH BELOW,
> BLOOD, FIRE, AND VAPOR OF SMOKE.
> [20] THE SUN WILL BE TURNED INTO DARKNESS
> AND THE MOON INTO BLOOD,
> BEFORE THE GREAT AND GLORIOUS DAY OF THE LORD COMES.
> [21] AND IT SHALL BE *THAT* EVERYONE WHO CALLS ON THE NAME OF THE LORD WILL BE SAVED.'

---

[32] these men (Amplified, NIV); these (ASV, KJV, NKJV)

God had been reticent during the period preceding the coming of Christ. Prophetic voices were relatively silent even before the time Alexander the Great (356-323 BC) entered the land. Still, the Israelites knew the Old Testament prophecies concerning the Messiah and many had heard John the Baptist's claim that the Messiah would soon be among them. Anticipation was so great at the time that some even questioned whether John was the Messiah (Luke 3: 15). Jerusalem was primed for the message that was delivered on the Day of Pentecost.

Not only had Peter answered the charge of drunkenness successfully, but his answer seemed to settle the crowd and draw their attention back to the apostles. The thunderous commotion along with the miracle of tongues initially brought the crowd together, and Peter's eloquence had trumped the allegations against the apostles as the people ended their chatter and yielded to his voice. That gave him the opportunity to offer the message God intended for him to deliver.

In diffusing the claim of intoxication, Peter first responded negatively in that he had explained what was *not* happening. Thus, he had answered that the apostles were not drunk. However, this did not resolve the crowd's initial question, which was, "What does this mean?" (v. 12). It was now on the shoulders of Peter and the other apostles to provide a fuller explanation. Having the attention of the throng of people (we can assume he was still speaking in other languages), Peter continued.

In his answer, Peter began by invoking the name of a well-known Israelite prophet. The apostle's words were clear and sure as he enlightened those in the crowd concerning the link between the events of the day and the words from the Old Testament prophet. By proclaiming, "this is what has been spoken through the prophet Joel" (v. 16), he was making the claim to his audience that they were witnessing the fulfillment of Old Testament prophecy.[33] Since these

---

[33] Certain scholars link the tongues of Pentecost with words found in Isaiah 28: 9-11. According to the prophet, the Israelites were essentially unteachable. They were even worse than little children to whom lessons had to be repeated consistently over time until they understood. In essence, they refused to learn. Because of their stubbornness and/or obtuseness, God would speak his message through foreign tongues, presumably in an effort to get them to pay attention.

The NIV Study Bible has a footnote on this for Isaiah 28:10. When prophesying that God would speak to them "with foreign lips and strange tongues," he makes the connection with their mockery in vs. 11. Also, when Paul is discussing the phenomenon of glossolalia at Corinth, he quotes Isaiah 28:10 as being fulfilled through this gift (1 Corinthians 14:21).

were *devout* Jews (v. 5), they would have heard Joel's prophecies as they were read in the temple on occasion. Peter's initial comment concerning the link to this prophecy would have brought the crowd into focus as they awaited further clarification.

The prophecy cited by Peter (Joel 2: 28-32) on this occasion, along with its eschatological implications, has been contemplated and analyzed by countless scholars for centuries. For instance, what did Joel mean by *the last days*? How would God pour out his Spirit on all mankind? What are we to think concerning *prophecies, visions,* and *dreams*? What *wonders* can we anticipate? What would be "the great and glorious day of the Lord?" (v. 20). Since these have been scrutinized and debated at length by a multitude of authors over hundreds of years, there is already much fodder available for the Bible student or aspiring biblical interpreter. A few comments here would not add significantly to the debate, so no attempt will be made at this time to reveal some previously undisclosed truth concerning these verses.

What we can discuss with confidence, however, is certain points from the prophecy upon which scholars generally agree. For instance, there is common acceptance that Joel's prophecy was not completely fulfilled on the Day of Pentecost. Therefore, Peter was not claiming that final fulfillment of the prophecy was realized on that day. What he was saying is that these Israelites were living at a time when prophecies such as this one concerning *the last days* were being fulfilled. Prophetic fulfillment was unfolding before their very eyes. They were living in *the last days* (most scholars consider this a reference to the church age) when those who seek the Lord, calling upon his name, will be saved.

The Israelites had a distinct view of what constituted *the last days*. They believed this to be a reference to the days of the Messiah. However, rather than a spiritual reign, they tended to believe that the Messiah would come to restore Israel on earth.[34]

Additionally, Joel had prophesied that God would "pour out my Spirit on all mankind" (v. 17). This statement must be considered within the scope of general scriptural context. First of all, most serious students of the Bible concur that this portion of Joel's prophecy saw

---

[34] *The phrase, "Last days," was used by the Jews to denote the last dispensation, that of Christ.* Johnson, B. W., The People's New Testament with Explanatory Notes, p. 419.

only partial fulfillment on the Day of Pentecost. To this point only the apostles had experienced the Spirit. When and how God would pour out his Spirit on mankind in general was as yet unknown.

The other important point to keep in mind when it comes to God pouring out his Spirit is that not every man and woman will receive God's Spirit. In their teachings, Jesus and the apostles mention certain qualifications (e.g., John 7: 38-39; 14: 15-17; Acts 2: 38; 5: 37; 1 Corinthians 2: 14) for those who seek to be honored by the presence of the Holy Spirit in their lives. Therefore, *all mankind* cannot mean that God would pour out his Spirit on each human being without exception. Consequently, *all mankind* must be a reference to either all nations (or nationalities) and/or generations. Given the many lessons of Scripture concerning the Spirit, we can say with conviction that God had both nationalities and generations in mind. He extends the gift of the Spirit to men even today and will continue offering the Spirit to all believers until Christ's return.

Perhaps Peter's most significant revelation to the crowd was the fact that he and the apostles were not responsible for the miracle these people were witnessing. The miracle was God's. Thus, he was able to divert attention away from himself and the other apostles and direct it toward the message that awaited those willing to listen. Once these Jews recognized that the miracle before them was from God, many opened their hearts and minds and gave honest consideration to the words Peter was about to say. They were ready to hear the message that God would deliver through the lips of the apostles.

Chapter 8

The Message

Acts 2: 22-36

> [22] "Men of Israel, listen to these words: Jesus the Nazarene, a Man attested to you by God with miracles and wonders and signs which God performed through Him in your midst, just as you yourselves know— [23] this *Man*, delivered over by the predetermined plan and foreknowledge of God, you nailed to a cross by the hands of godless men and put *Him* to death. [24] But God raised Him *from the dead*, putting an end to the agony of death, since it was impossible for Him to be held in its power.

Peter's words concerning the prophet Joel provided an introduction to the homily he ultimately delivered. The citation from the prophet offered a context for the meat of the message. While the crowd now understood that they were witnessing fulfillment of prophecy, their question concerning the meaning of these things had not yet been answered, so they must have remained bewildered.

The reference to "Men of Israel" (v. 22) in such an open setting, does not mean that Peter's audience consisted only of Israelite men. On a public stage like this, it would be essentially impossible to gather such a crowd without including women and children. We find that when Philip was in Samaria, where a similar gathering is described, both men and women responded to the evangelist's words (Acts 8: 12). We can safely assume that Peter was addressing men and women, young and old, in such a tremendous gathering.

The people of Jerusalem were not unfamiliar with Jesus. It had been less than two months since that fateful day when he hung on the cross, the midday sky turned to darkness, the earth shook, and the curtain of the temple was torn (Matthew 27: 45-51). Even those who were not present for the crucifixion would have been aware of the circumstances surrounding his death. Human nature dictates that talk of Jesus would have continued well beyond the crucifixion itself, especially with the apostles and one hundred twenty disciples in town. While the chatter concerning Jesus may have leveled off, it was undoubtedly still a big deal in conversations around Jerusalem.

In remarkably few words, Peter laid the peoples' sin at their own feet. He recalled for them the good things Jesus had done in their midst including signs and wonders that, according to the apostle, provided testimony from God as to Jesus' true identity. Peter would not allow them to plead ignorance. He proclaimed that they were fully aware of the things Jesus had done.

Yet, with full knowledge and forethought, they sought Jesus' death. They even went so far as to release Barabbas, a criminal, instead of Jesus, when given the choice (Matthew 27: 15-26). The truth that all of this was preordained by God, and the fact that they may have been unduly influenced by the chief priests and elders, did not release these Israelites from responsibility for what had occurred.

This statement by Peter indicates that what had taken place resulted from God's design of that which was necessary to free men from sin in complement with the free will of men. Yet, this creates a difficult paradox. Some may consider these concepts contradictory, suggesting that a plan designed and preordained by God cannot be carried out via man's free will, but God does not see it that way. Peter's words are clear that the Israelites were *responsible* for Christ's death even in the presence of God's foreknowledge and design. This indicates that the Israelites might have avoided crucifying Christ, but God knew the choice they would make. The Geneva Study Bible states it thusly:

> God's counsel doth not excuse the Jews, whose hands were wicked. The fault is said to be theirs, by whose counsel and egging forward it was done.[35]

Similarly, they were not relieved of guilt simply because they had turned Jesus over to *godless men* (Gentiles) for execution. Pilate even admitted finding no fault in him saying, "What evil has he done?" (Matthew 27: 23). The narrative suggests that Pilate would have preferred to release Jesus, but chose instead to please the crowd, ineffectually washing his hands of the decision that was made (Matthew 27: 24).

What would have kept Jesus' name at the forefront in the minds and conversations of the Jews over the preceding weeks was the fact of his resurrection. The chief priests and elders had bribed the soldiers

---

[35] Lilliback, Peter A., Advisory Board Chairman, 1599 Geneva Bible Restoration Project, <u>1599 Geneva Bible, Tolle Lege Press</u>, p. 1094.

who had been guarding the tomb so that they would lie about the resurrection, claiming that Jesus' disciples had stolen the body while the soldiers slept (Matthew 28: 12-15), but there were too many witnesses to keep the truth of the resurrection completely hidden. Additionally, we are told that when Jesus died, a host of saints who had previously passed from this life rose from the dead. After Jesus' resurrection they entered the city of Jerusalem and appeared to a number of people there (Matthew 27: 50-53). We do not know what happened to these risen souls afterward, but such an event would have been both thrilling and frightening for the citizens of Jerusalem who witnessed it. Therefore, it would have continued as a topic of conversation even these many weeks later.

When Peter raised the issue of Jesus' resurrection, it must have struck a nerve. All the murmurings in shops and on street corners, which had probably been dismissed as pure myth by many of the Israelites, were true, and Peter's audience knew it even if they had been unwilling to admit it to themselves. Jesus was the Son of God. The fact that he was sent from God was substantiated by the signs and wonders he had performed. As the Son of God, he could not be constrained even by death. Now the claim had been spoken publicly in the midst of a miracle of untold measure. This would make the balance of Peter's message difficult for these Jews to ignore.

[25] For David says of Him,

'I SAW THE LORD CONTINUALLY BEFORE ME,
BECAUSE HE IS AT MY RIGHT HAND, SO THAT I WILL NOT BE SHAKEN.
[26] THEREFORE MY HEART WAS GLAD AND MY TONGUE WAS OVERJOYED;
MOREOVER MY FLESH ALSO WILL LIVE IN HOPE;
[27] FOR YOU WILL NOT ABANDON MY SOUL TO HADES,
NOR WILL YOU ALLOW YOUR HOLY ONE TO UNDERGO DECAY.
[28] YOU HAVE MADE KNOWN TO ME THE WAYS OF LIFE;
YOU WILL MAKE ME FULL OF GLADNESS WITH YOUR PRESENCE.'

The measure of prophetic fulfillment over the weeks leading up to and including the Day of Pentecost was staggering, partly because it was multi-dimensional (e.g., each apostle spoke numerous foreign languages simultaneously) and partly because these people were living through and witnessing the fulfillment of multiple prophecies. Before them was what Peter described as fulfillment of Joel's prophecy, but the apostle was not finished citing the Old Testament prophets.

David, who ruled over Israel from 1055-1015 BC, had a special bond with God. So extraordinary was their relationship that God considered him "...a man after His own heart" (1 Samuel 13: 14). He was one of the most admired men in Israelite history, ranking, in the minds of most first-century Jews, with men like Abraham and Moses. Yet David was not merely a king. He was also a prophet of God. The many Psalms he wrote hold an abundance of prophetic utterances.

As evidence of the truth of Jesus' resurrection, including the fact that it happened with God's full foreknowledge, Peter turned to these words from King David (Psalm 16: 8-11). His sermon to the crowd was calculated and efficient, which is not surprising given the fact that he was inspired by the Holy Spirit. While they likely hung on every word Peter spoke, if he had begun to lose the attention of any of his listeners, invoking the name of David would have drawn them back.

The name of Jesus (vs. 22-24) served as the antecedent for "THE LORD" (v. 24) mentioned in David's proclamation as part of Peter's address. What did David have to say about Jesus, according to the apostle? The Psalm cited by Peter was a treatise about David's relationship with the Lord and how he revered him. Within those words, David provided Peter the evidence he required concerning Jesus' identity as the resurrected Messiah. As devout Jews, those in the crowd would not question David's words, and they did not question their application to Jesus, since no taunting is mentioned by Luke.

When David claimed that the Lord was "CONTINUALLY BEFORE ME" (v. 25), the expression may be viewed from two perspectives. As an equal within the Godhead, Jesus has the capacity to be where he wishes when he wishes. Indeed, he can be everywhere since he shares the attribute of omnipresence with the Father and the Spirit. Therefore, being with him *continually* is not an embellishment on David's part. Jesus could, indeed, be with David anytime and anywhere.

At the same time, the remark says much about David himself, indicating that his mind was always fixed on the Lord. In fact, this is probably a more accurate interpretation of the thought David intended to convey. Where David went, he took the Lord with him. His mind was always focused on the things of God as he sought to please him. Thus, the Lord was always in his presence.

Having the Lord by his side at all times and in every circumstance allowed David to walk with confidence among men, knowing that his bond with the Lord was sure. He was not shaken by earthly events. In fact, the moment in David's life when he was most visibly distraught was when he realized that, by his own sin, he had jeopardized the life of his own son (2 Samuel 12: 13-23).

David not only took the Lord with him wherever he went, but he took pleasure in that thought. It was probably not unusual for David to blurt out a Hebrew *praise the Lord*, exalting the Lord with his tongue (v. 26) simply because of the enjoyment he experienced by having the Lord in his life. He not only found pleasure in his union with the Lord, but he also found hope there, knowing there was life beyond this physical realm.

Having offered the setting, Peter cited some words concerning a resurrection, and those words linked David's prophecy to the events about which Peter was speaking. David had proclaimed, "FOR YOU WILL NOT ABANDON MY SOUL TO HADES, NOR WILL YOU ALLOW YOUR HOLY ONE TO UNDERGO DECAY" (v. 27). Prophesying from the Lord's perspective as in the first person, David foretold the resurrection of the "HOLY ONE."

> [29] "Brothers, I may confidently say to you regarding the patriarch David that he both died and was buried, and his tomb is with us to this day. [30] So because he was a prophet and knew that God had sworn to him with an oath to seat *one* of his descendants on his throne, [31] he looked ahead and spoke of the resurrection of the Christ, that He was neither abandoned to Hades, nor did His flesh suffer decay.

Peter continued his discourse concerning King David, since he played such a key role in the events of the day. Although David had been dead for more than one thousand years, stories about him held deep meaning for the Israelites. Surprisingly, Peter's first move was to acknowledge that David was dead and buried. It is believed his tomb was located somewhere beyond the wall on the south side of the current city of Jerusalem. This is where the *city of David* would have been located. Many may have even turned their heads in the direction of David's tomb as Peter spoke, contemplating his burial site.

More than a millennium had passed since God made a certain promise to David. God had promised him that his descendant would be king of the Jews. Of course, David had many descendants who filled the role of king over the Jewish nation. However, it was clear to David that this promise involved much more than mere kingship. What he referred to was not an earthly throne, but the throne of God. This was an oath concerning the promised Messiah. God promised, and David prophesied, that he would come through the lineage of David.

³² *It is* this Jesus *whom* God raised up, *a fact* to which we are all witnesses. ³³ Therefore, since He has been exalted at the right hand of God, and has received the promise of the Holy Spirit from the Father, He has poured out this which you both see and hear. ³⁴ For it was not David who ascended into heaven, but he himself says:

'The Lord said to my Lord,
"Sit at My right hand,
³⁵ Until I make Your enemies a footstool for Your feet."'

³⁶ Therefore let all the house of Israel know for certain that God has made Him both Lord and Christ—this Jesus whom you crucified."

The crowd that encircled Peter and the apostles had originally inquired about the meaning of the spectacle before them as the apostles spoke in numerous tongues (v. 12). In answer to their question, Peter had addressed much more than the miracle of languages that had drawn them in and presented for them the broader picture concerning the meaning of these things.

In answering their question, Peter first considered the prophets of old, declaring that they were, indeed, witnessing fulfillment of that which was foretold in Old Testament prophecies. He began by citing Joel and his prophecies concerning the many wonders men would see in the last days (vs. 16-21). They were now witnessing fulfillment of the things Joel had foreseen. While this may have shed some light, it did not satisfy the heart of their query. The fact that they were witnessing prophecy fulfilled helped them to understand *what* was happening. It did not, however, help them to understand *why* this was happening. Therefore, Peter continued.

Having explained *what* was taking place, which was fulfillment of Joel's predictions, Peter offered the *reason* these things were now coming to pass. Pointing to David, the apostle explained that what they were witnessing involved much more than the miracle that was currently before them. Jesus of Nazareth, a man who came from God, which was evident from the miracles he had performed, and whom they had crucified just seven weeks earlier, was raised from the dead by the hand of God (vs. 22-24). Jesus was, according to Peter, a man of such standing that even the grave could not contain him. David had prophesied concerning Jesus' death and resurrection (vs. 25-31). Jesus was a promise fulfilled (v. 30).

Finally, Peter came full circle. He laid the heart of his message at the feet of these devout Jews. This Jesus, whom they had so willingly offered up, had risen from the dead, as prophesied, and the apostles were witnesses to that fact (v. 32). Having risen from the grave, Jesus had ascended to heaven where he sat at God's right hand, which was fulfillment of another of David's prophecies (vs. 34-35). In Jesus' stead, as they awaited his return, God sent the promised Holy Spirit. According to the apostle, God had *poured out* his Spirit, in keeping with the prophecy from Joel (v. 18). The tongues they spoke were intended as a demonstration of the power of the Spirit so the Jews would accept that the apostles were, indeed, God's spokesmen. How else could they do something that was so far beyond their abilities?

Given all that had occurred over the past few weeks, the Jews in Jerusalem had reason to take Peter's words at face value. The rumors concerning Jesus' resurrection were true. It is likely many of the Jews in Jerusalem had been remorseful over their treatment of Jesus, although they probably believed they could do nothing to atone for their actions. Therefore, they simply held on to their guilt. Yet, if there was no way to atone for their sin, why were these apostles standing before them on God's behalf? Perhaps…just perhaps…God was offering them an opportunity for redemption.

Chapter 9

The Response

Acts 2: 37-41

³⁷ Now when they heard *this*, they were pierced to the heart, and said to Peter and the rest of the apostles, "Brothers, what are we to do?"

As we observe the reaction from the crowd, it is fascinating to note that they responded directly to the apostles. They did not address the one hundred twenty believers, as though these disciples were equally engaged in delivering God's message. The people targeted the apostles only. This is very telling, suggesting that something very obvious about the apostles distinguished them from all others on that day.

It was from the apostles that they had heard God's message proclaimed from the beginning. It was the apostles who had addressed each man in his native tongue. While the evidence was already overwhelming, Luke has provided even further evidence here to support the position that the Spirit fell only upon the apostles and they, in turn, spoke in tongues on that day (vs. 1-4).

Peter's sermon on the Day of Pentecost was concise, but it was also powerful, fortified by the presence of the Holy Spirit. It quickly became obvious to those listening that the prophecy they had heard so many times in the temple readings had now been fulfilled in the person of Jesus. That is probably because many people were already somewhat convicted in their hearts concerning Jesus' death. That is not to say that they recognized him as the Messiah, but they knew he had not deserved the death he had suffered. He was a good teacher who had performed miracles throughout the land.

We cannot dismiss the influence of the Holy Spirit on the crowd that day. The fact that these were devout Jews (v. 5) suggests that they were eager to hear and accept godly teachings. These were people who would want God to work on their hearts and convict them of their sins. Thus, it is possible that the Spirit intervened on their behalf and opened their hearts so that they would believe the words of the apostles. Now their eyes were opened, and they understood that Jesus was, in fact, the promised Messiah.

Peter exclaimed, per Joel's prophecy, that "in the last days... everyone who calls on the name of the Lord will be saved" (vs. 17, 21). Although Peter was citing the prophet, the prophecy itself does not clarify what it means to *call on the name of the Lord*, and the apostle does not offer additional insight during his sermon concerning this expression. This lack of illumination explains the crowd's response at the end of Peter's sermon as they asked, "Brethren, what are we to do?" (v. 37).

It is apparent from their question that those who asked it believed the message the apostles had presented. Luke states that "they were pierced to the heart" (v. 37). They knew they were guilty of sinning against God and now sought redemption. Peter had just explained to them that they were now in the last days when those who would call on the Lord would be saved. From their query, then, we understand that they wanted to know *how* they might call upon his name.

> **38** Peter *said* to them, "Repent, and each of you be baptized in the name of Jesus Christ for the forgiveness of your sins; and you will receive the gift of the Holy Spirit.

Often when the disciples asked Jesus questions, he responded with what might be considered vague answers. Much of Jesus' teachings were given through parables with at least partially hidden meanings. In fact, Jesus taught via the use of parables so often that it led his followers to ask, "Why do you speak to them in parables?" (Matthew 13: 10). They could not understand why he did not simply offer straightforward answers and instead, sought to teach lessons with deeper spiritual meaning. Jesus' reason for the parables was that some were not ready to understand deep spiritual principles and certain heavenly secrets must wait for the appropriate time to be revealed.

Unlike the abstract nature of Jesus' parables, Peter's reply in this situation is uncomplicated. He understood that they had reached the moment for the secrets of the kingdom to be revealed to all men. When the crowd asked, *"what are we to do?"* the apostle's first answer was that they should *repent*.

Strictly speaking, the word *repent* signifies a change of mindset.[36] However, we can infer much more about this word from the manner in

---

[36] *3340.* μετανοεω **metanoeo**, *met-an-o-eh'-o*; from *3326* and *3539*; to *think differently* or *afterwards*, i.e. reconsider (mor. feel *compunction*):--repent. Strong,

which the idea of repentance is presented within the pages of Scripture. When Peter told those in the crowd to repent, as with countless other passages, the idea of repentance eclipses a mere change of mind and encompasses a change of heart – an attitude of remorse for thoughts and actions that had separated them from God.

Repentance involves more than simply recognizing that one has sinned. It entails viewing sin as God sees sin. The man who seeks to honor God will lament over his own sins with what Paul termed "godly sorrow" (2 Corinthians 7: 10, NIV), knowing that by his actions he has grieved the heart of God. Then, having examined those actions as God would view them, his natural response would be to turn from those kinds of actions (change of mind and heart) because he treasures God and does not wish to cause him sorrow. That is the essence of repentance as it is addressed in God's Word.

Peter told the people to repent, but he did not stop there. Not only were they to repent, but they were to "be baptized in the name of Jesus Christ" (v. 38). The people understood what Peter meant when he said *be baptized* (immersed).[37] For the Israelites, the use of water for spiritual purification reaches back to Old Testament times and the rituals defined in the Abrahamic covenant. They had also witnessed the baptism performed by John the Baptist, called "…a baptism of repentance for the forgiveness of sins" (Luke 3: 3).

What distinguished the baptism commanded by Peter was the fact that it was to be done "in the name of Jesus Christ" (v. 38). This was new. Baptism in Jesus' name (or by the authority of his name) was established by Christ in what is known as the Great Commission.

> [18] And Jesus came up and spoke to them, saying, "All authority in heaven and on earth has been given to Me. [19] Go, therefore, and make disciples of all the nations, baptizing them in the name of the Father and the Son and the Holy Spirit, [20] teaching them to follow all that I commanded you; and behold, I am with you always, to the end of the age." (Matthew 28: 18-20)

James, The New Exhaustive Concordance of the Bible-Dictionary of the Greek Testament, p. 47.

[37] 907. βαπτιζω **baptizo**, *bap-tid'-zo*; from a der. of *911*; to *make whelmed* (i.e. *fully wet*); used only (in the N.T.) of ceremonial *ablution*, espec. (techn.) of the ordinance of Chr. *baptism*:--baptist, baptize, wash. Ibid, p. 18.

Why were these people to repent and be baptized? According to Peter's words, it was *for forgiveness of their sins*. The word translated *for*[38] portrays their repentance and submission to baptism as *leading to*, or *resulting in*, forgiveness. Thus, the apostles were commanding the people exactly as Jesus had instructed them when he said, "make disciples of all nations, baptizing them" (Matthew 28: 19). However, baptism was ineffectual without repentance. They were to repent *and* be baptized in order to experience the redemption they sought.

Peter had answered their question succinctly and unambiguously. However, what came next must have been a pleasant surprise for those present. According to the apostle, those who heeded his words, that is, those who repented and submitted to baptism, would receive an additional blessing. They would receive what Peter described as "the gift of the Holy Spirit" (v. 38). That is not to say they would speak in tongues like the apostles. As we understand the *gift* of the Spirit, as it is portrayed in the Bible, it differs from the *gifts* of the Spirit such as tongues.

The apostles taught that the Holy Spirit abides with those who belong to Christ (Romans 8: 9; 1 Corinthians 3: 16; 1 John 4: 13), providing insight into Peter's proclamation concerning the gift of the Spirit and what it means for the person with whom the Holy Spirit dwells. Yet not all believers spoke in tongues (1 Corinthians 12: 30). Therefore, the Holy Spirit does not always manifest himself in miraculous gifts such as tongues. Nonetheless, Peter's words are clear that those who repented and were baptized would, indeed, realize this presence of the Holy Spirit in their lives.

B. W. Johnson, a theologian from the nineteenth century, summarized this verse in these words:

> 38. Repent, and be baptized. For the first time the terms of pardon under the New Covenant and the Great Commission are given; given once for all

---

[38] *1519.* εισ **eis**, *ice*; a prim. prep.; *to* or *into* (indicating the point reached or entered), of place, time, or (fig.) purpose (result, etc.); also in adv. phrases: -- [abundant-] ly, against, among, as, at, [back-] ward, before, by, concerning, + continual, + far more exceeding, for [intent, purpose], fore, + forth, in (among, at unto, -so much that, -to), to the intent that, + of one mind, + never, of, (up-) on, + perish, + set at one again, (so) that, therefore (-unto), throughout, till, to (be, the end, -ward), (here-) until (-to), . . . ward, [where-] fore, with. Often used in composition with the same general import, but only with verbs (etc.) expressing motion (lit. or fig.). Ibid, p. 26.

time, and always the same. The convicted, broken-hearted, sorrowing sinner, believing that Jesus is the Christ, is to repent and be baptized. Repent. Not sorrow. They already sorrowed; but a change of purpose; the internal change which resolves to serve the Lord. The Greek term rendered repent, means a change of mind. The act of obedience in baptism is an outward expression of both faith and repentance. In the name of Jesus Christ. "Upon the name" (Revised Version). Upon the ground of the name. In submission to the authority of Jesus Christ. For the remission of sins. Thus, by complying with the conditions just named, they shall receive remission of sins. No man can receive pardon without faith and repentance, nor can he without submission to the will of Christ. "Eis (for) denotes the object of baptism, which is the remission of the guilt contracted in the state before metanoia (repentance)."--Meyer. "In order to the forgiveness of sins we connect naturally with both the preceding verbs. This clause states the motive or object which should induce them to repent and be baptized."--*Prof. Hackett*. The gift of the Holy Spirit. Promised as a comforter to all who obey Christ, but whom "the world cannot receive."[39]

With his words on the Day of Pentecost, Peter had offered the initial presentation of the gospel message in the church age. This is the message that Paul insisted would remain unaltered (Galatians 1: 8-9). It is the message Jesus had given the apostles that they were to share with men of all nations. The crowd had received their answer to the question, "Brethren, what are we to do?" (v. 38). They now knew how to "call upon the name of the Lord" (v. 21).

However, having preached the first gospel message, and having delivered an extraordinarily direct answer to the one question that would eventually be asked by everyone who wished to honor God (what are we to do?), Peter was not finished.

[39] "For the promise is for you and your children and for all who are far away, as many as the Lord our God will call to Himself."

The apostle explained that the last days involved more than this one day and this special miracle (vs. 17-21). He continued to enlighten the crowd. Those things of which he spoke encompassed much more than the households represented in Jerusalem on that day. The promise was not limited to them simply because they happened to be in Jerusalem at a specific day and time to celebrate a Jewish festival. Instead, Peter proclaimed that the promise was for them and their children. It was even for those who lived in distant lands.

---

[39] Johnson, B. W., The People's New Testament with Explanatory Notes, p. 424.

While it was Peter who spoke these words, he was speaking by the power of the Holy Spirit. Therefore, even Peter may not have grasped the universal impact of his words. Later he had to be convinced, through a vision and the miracle of tongues bestowed on Cornelius and those with him in Caesarea (Acts 10: 9-34), that the gospel message would also apply to Gentiles. Nonetheless, his hearers understood that a new day had dawned in their relationship with God.

The promise was for all men, both near and far. It was for their children and their children's children. It was meant for those nearby as well as those in far-off lands. The promise was all-embracing in that it was intended for all men everywhere throughout the ages to come.

Some may wonder what implications such a statement might have on the baptism of infants. Did Peter mean, when he said, "the promise is for you and your children," that infants should be baptized? If that is the case, it seems to conflict with the relationship that Peter established in the previous verse where he stated that, by a combination of repentance and baptism a man's sin may be forgiven.

Peter was not pointing to newborn babies with these words. What Peter had in mind was generations, not infants. He was stating that this was a promise that would stand for all generations to come. That is to say, the promise applied to those in the crowd as well as their descendants. It applied to those who were far off both in time and space.

Exactly what promise could apply to such a vast array that it encompassed both nations and generations? It was the very promise Peter had just made.

> [38] Peter *said* to them, "Repent, and each of you be baptized in the name of Jesus Christ for the forgiveness of your sins; and you will receive the gift of the Holy Spirit.

The promise was twofold. First, they were promised forgiveness of their sins. As an additional blessing, however, they were promised the presence of the Holy Spirit as a comforter (John 14: 16) and teacher (John 14: 26) in their lives. Yet, these promises were not unconditional. They were connected directly with the commands Peter had set forth. Therefore, a man's opportunity to realize the fulfillment of these promises relied upon his obedience to those commands. They were to repent and be baptized.

⁴⁰ And with many other words he solemnly testified and kept on urging them, saying, "Be saved from this perverse generation!"

To this point Peter's sermon was the epitome of brevity. So much information in so few words undoubtedly left his listeners with a lot of questions, and quizzical facial expressions must have permeated the crowd. However, Peter had much more to say. He continued speaking, explaining that Jesus' blood was the cleansing agent for their sins and the means by which they could be reconciled to God. He taught them that Jesus was the means by which they could know eternal life. "With many other words" (v. 40) he taught them the way of salvation. Luke cites a small portion of the words spoken on that day, but it is possible that the sermon continued for a considerable length of time as Peter and the apostles offered even more insight into the gospel message.

Peter's sermon, as he "kept on urging[40] them" (v. 40), would have consisted of a combination of encouraging thoughts and concern for their souls as he stressed the urgency of the situation along with the blessings that awaited them. He may have thrown in, as a matter of explanation, that they now had an opportunity that was unavailable in the Abrahamic covenant. In the end, it was all about salvation. Peter pleaded with them to choose salvation.

⁴¹ So then, those who had received his word were baptized; and that day there were added about three thousand souls.

When Peter had finished speaking, his listeners felt the powerful impact from his words. They were guilty without excuse. They obviously took Peter's words seriously, realizing that not only had they crucified the promised Messiah, but they were separated from God by their countless sins against him. Consequently, the conviction of those in the crowd manifested itself in a massive response to Peter's challenge.

While it is difficult to estimate exactly how many Jews were in Jerusalem on that fateful day, or how many were listening to Peter and the other apostles, we know that the population of the city naturally

---

[40] *3870. παρακαλεω* **parakaleo**, *par-ak-al-eh'-o*; from *3844* and *2564*; to *call near*, i.e. *invite, invoke* (by *imploration, hortation* or *consolation*):--beseech, call for, (be of good) comfort, desire, (give) exhort (-ation), intreat, pray. Strong, James, The New Exhaustive Concordance of the Bible-Dictionary of the Greek Testament, p. 335.

tended to swell at the time of the feast. We can surmise from the narrative that the number ranged somewhere in the thousands since, according to Luke, about three thousand of those present responded positively to Peter's words.

How did these people act in response to the gospel message that was presented on that day? They responded as Peter had commanded them when they asked, "Brethren, what are we to do?" They repented and were baptized in the name of Jesus Christ (v. 38). Although we are not expressly told of their repentance in the narrative, they were, that day, counted among the believers. Given the fact that Peter had established both repentance and baptism as requirements, accompanied by the fact that "they were pierced to the heart," we can safely presume that they responded according to Peter's instructions. That is to say, they repented and submitted to baptism.

Having responded according to apostolic instruction, we can be assured that those who believed that day also experienced those things Peter had offered up in the message. They were, as promised, forgiven of their sins and, as a result of their faithfulness, received the blessing of the Holy Spirit as a constant companion (v. 38).

Thus, the church was born on the Day of Pentecost. The body of believers whom Jesus had envisioned would embrace his teachings and would ultimately constitute the kingdom of God on earth that was established on that day. This was the kingdom of God that Jesus had depicted in the many parables he had shared throughout his ministry on earth. And yet, the work of the Holy Spirit and the ministry of the apostles had only just begun.

Chapter 10

The Aftermath

Acts 2: 42-47

[42] They were continually devoting themselves to the apostles' teaching and to fellowship, to the breaking of bread and to prayer.

Peter's sermon on the Day of Pentecost was powerful. Thousands of men and women joined them as believers on that day. However, the saga did not end there. The Day of Pentecost was the beginning of a journey for the apostles. Jesus had assigned them a precise role when he spoke the Great Commission (Matthew 28: 19-20) that was mentioned in the previous chapter (see page 66).

The apostles were to "...make disciples of all nations, baptizing them..." (Matthew 28: 19). Making disciples meant offering initial instruction concerning Jesus as the Messiah and his sacrifice for our sins (Romans 10: 14) and convincing people of the truth of that message such that they would choose to accept Jesus and receive forgiveness via repentance and baptism. This is what had begun on the Day of Pentecost. The apostles had proclaimed the gospel message and, in making them disciples, three thousand were baptized.

Peter's words on the Day of Pentecost were very thorough regarding the gospel message of salvation. Still, there was much more to teach. Through his teachings during his ministry on earth Jesus sought to depict for men the distinctiveness God desired to see in those who wished to have a relationship with him. He sought to teach that having fellowship with God in the new covenant was no longer about obedience to the details of the Mosaic Law. Instead, God desires for people to have a personal relationship with him and reflect godly attributes in their daily lives.

Jesus had provided considerable instruction to the apostles when it came to guiding those who chose to accept him as Savior. The apostles were commissioned to instruct them "...to observe all that I commanded you" (Matthew 28: 20). Christianity was not just about believing in Jesus, repenting, and being baptized for the forgiveness of sins. In order to *observe* (hold fast to)[41] all that Jesus had commanded, they needed to *learn* all that he had commanded. Much more instruction would be necessary if those who believed were to become the kind of people God wanted them to be. Thus, apostolic instruction continued beyond the Day of Pentecost for those who accepted Jesus as their Savior.

The apostles committed themselves to teaching and the disciples devoted themselves "to the apostles' teaching" (v. 42). They took seriously the apostles' instructions and sought to follow their directions concerning how they ought to live their lives.

These new Christians also committed to fellowshipping with one another and with God. A key element of a man's relationship with God is found in his relationship with other believers. Fellowshipping together would have involved coming together and worshipping God corporately as well as serving each other by meeting the needs, both physical and spiritual, of their fellow Christians.

The phrase "breaking of bread" (v. 42) is known to carry two distinct meanings in New Testament writings. It can be a reference to partaking of the Lord's Supper (Acts 20: 7; 1 Corinthians 10: 16) for spiritual sustenance, but it can also be used to depict men simply sitting down to a meal (Luke 24: 30, 35; Acts 27: 35) for physical nourishment. In this case, the former appears to be in play. It is unlikely that Luke would offer up casual dining in the midst of a narrative that focuses on the spiritual elements of the early church (i.e., the apostles' teaching, fellowship, and prayer). While the narrative does not inform us exactly how often they partook of the Lord's Supper, Paul later explained that the members of the body gathered for the Lord's Supper on the first day of the week (Acts 20: 7). Scholars generally agree that this was intended to recognize and honor the day of Jesus' resurrection (Luke 24: 1-8).

Finally, the disciples devoted themselves to prayer. It is likely that Luke has in mind not just corporate prayer, which was a major part of

---

[41] *5083.* τφρεω **tereo**, *tay-reh'-o*; from **teros** (*a watch*; perh. akin to *2334*); to *guard* (from *loss* or *injury*, prop. by keeping *the eye* upon; and thus differing from *5442*, which is prop. to *prevent* escaping; and from *2892*, which implies a *fortress* or full military lines of apparatus), i.e. to *note* (a prophecy; fig. to *fulfil* a command); by impl. to *detain* (in custody; fig. to *maintain*); by extens. to *withhold* (for personal ends; fig. to keep *unmarried*):--hold fast, keep (-er), (ob-, pre-, re) serve, watch. Ibid,, p. 71.

their fellowship together, but also the personal prayer lives of the believers as they sought to develop a deeper relationship with God. The apostles would have encouraged the kind of prayer life they saw in Jesus. This same kind of prayer life would have been demonstrated in the lives of the apostles.

> [43] Everyone kept feeling a sense of awe; and many wonders and signs were taking place through the apostles.

Some versions translate *awe* as *fear*[42] in this passage. Both words probably apply to some degree, but *fear* is the more accurate interpretation. The believers had less reason to fear than those outside of Christ, but they still demonstrated severe reverence and a measure of fear toward the Lord. Similarly, those outside of Christ must have seriously considered what was happening as they saw changes in the lives of the believers. Therefore, *everyone* likely refers to those both inside and outside the body of believers.

The world had never seen such a sense of unity among a group of people. They were unified in their love for Christ and for one another. They were united in their goal to bring others into the fold through the preaching of the gospel message. They devoted themselves to the things of God.

Adding to the amazement, and undoubtedly cultivating fear and inspiration among the people, was the fact that the apostles performed many powerful acts (wonders and signs). Prior to his ascension Jesus had promised the apostles that they would receive power (*dunamis*)[43] when the Holy Spirit came upon them. We saw a certain element of that power on the day of Pentecost when they spoke in strange tongues and were heard by those in the crowd, each in his own language (v. 8). Afterward, the apostles performed numerous miracles including healing the sick, for which they became well-known (Acts 5: 15).

Like the miracle of tongues, other miracles performed by the apostles were intended to give them standing before those with whom they shared the gospel message. The working of miracles helped to

---

[42] awe (NIV); fear (ASV, KJV, NKJV)

[43] *1411.* δυναμιϖ **dunamis**, *doo'-nam-is*; from *1410*; *force* (lit. or fig.); spec. miraculous *power* (usually by impl. a miracle itself):--ability, abundance, meaning, might (-ily, -y, -y deed), (worker of) miracle (-s), power, strength, violence, mighty (wonderful) work. Ibid, p. 24.

establish the church of the first century. These *signs and wonders* proved to unbelievers that the apostles stood before them on God's behalf. They were his representatives. Their words were to be believed and their instructions followed. These miracles, provided as proof of the apostles' authority, would have been cause for those outside of Christ to experience fear, knowing they were not following the apostles' lead.

Note that the working of miracles was limited to the apostles at this time. No others are portrayed as performing miracles until after the apostles laid hands on them. In fact, if we consider biblical accounts of these gifts candidly, it becomes clear that one special power the apostles possessed was the ability to distribute spiritual gifts to other believers. For instance, after the apostles laid their hands on the seven servants, Stephen and Phillip, who were among them, were able to perform miracles (Acts 6: 5-8; 8: 5-7).

As we consider biblical narrative, we discover that the ability to distribute spiritual gifts was limited to the apostles. Others often experienced miraculous spiritual gifts through the touch of the apostles, but those who received these gifts did not, in turn, distribute them to others. For instance, Phillip went to Samaria where he performed miracles and baptized those who responded to the gospel. However, it was only when the apostles (Peter and John) arrived and laid hands on the Samaritans that they, too, received spiritual gifts (Acts 8: 14-24).

This was a result of the power received on the Day of Pentecost by the apostles as the Spirit came upon them (1: 1-4). Similarly, Paul, who was appointed as an apostle much later and, consequently, received power from the Holy Spirit at a later date, told the Romans that he would love to come and see them and bestow them with spiritual gifts (Romans 1: 11). While it was the Spirit who distributed spiritual gifts among the believers (1 Corinthians 12: 11), the hands of the apostles were the tools through which those gifts were given.

The only exception to this principle was the case of Cornelius, who was the first Gentile to become a Christian (Acts 10: 34-48). The Holy Spirit fell upon Cornelius and those with him, and they began to speak in tongues as the apostles had done on Pentecost while Peter witnessed the event. Peter was quite surprised by the incident. What made the occasion so unique in Peter's eyes was the fact that 1) spiritual gifts had been given to the Gentiles and 2) these gifts had been given without an apostle's touch. Therefore, just as the tongues of the apostles had served as a sign to unbelievers on the Day of Pentecost, so the tongues among the Gentiles at the house of Cornelius served as a sign to Peter and those with him that salvation was not limited to the Jews, but was meant for the Gentiles as well (Acts 15: 8).

> [44] And all the believers were together and had all things in common; [45] and they would sell their property and possessions and share them with all, to the extent that anyone had need.

In the earliest days of the church those who followed Christ were seen sharing all they had with their brothers and sisters in Christ. The Mosaic Law commanded the people to care for those in need. They were commanded to be generous and openhanded to their fellow Jews (Deuteronomy 15: 7-11). At the heart of this teaching lies what Jesus deemed to be the second greatest commandment, which was, "You shall love your neighbor as yourself" (Mathew 22: 39).

The irony is that, while the Mosaic Law commanded the Jews to care for each others' needs, it was a commandment that was essentially ignored. Noticeably, the Pharisees neglected the poor, focusing mostly on themselves and their thirst for human recognition. When they gave alms to the poor or did anything else that seemed noble, their hidden agenda was self-aggrandizement (Matthew 23: 5).

In contrast, these early Christians shared all they had, not because it was commanded or because they sought the approval of men, but because it was their desire. Through the teaching of the apostles, they came to understand the unselfish character of Christ who had offered himself as a sacrifice for the sins of men. They understood that if they were to be like Christ, who was their model, they would need to walk as he walked. Serving Christ was accomplished by serving others and meeting their needs.

Not only did these early Christians care for each others' needs, but some sold off their capital assets, such as land, offering the money to help meet the needs of those among them who were less fortunate. There was a certain man named Barnabas who was a prime example of selflessness in the church when he sold some property and offered the money to the apostles (Acts 4: 36-37).

> [46] Day by day continuing with one mind in the temple, and breaking bread from house to house, they were taking their meals together with gladness and sincerity of heart, [47] praising God and having favor with all the people. And the Lord was adding to their number day by day those who were being saved.

The apostles must have spent much of their time teaching as they had been commissioned by Jesus (Matthew 28: 19-20), and the people listened intently, desiring to learn all they could about their Savior and what was expected from them in the life they had chosen. Thus, they spent considerable time together. When they were not at work or taking care of chores and other domestic duties, they sought out the apostles, who were normally at the temple, or fellow Christians for worship and fellowship.

They did not live communally since they departed to their various homes for meals. Given the context, breaking of bread, in this instance, most likely points to the disciples sharing regular meals together as opposed to Luke's earlier reference to the Lord's Supper (v. 42). They were invited into each others' homes for various meals. This was another opportunity to share, and they obviously took advantage of it. In all likelihood, those who were in need were invited into the homes of those who were blessed with great abundance. All of this was done cheerfully as they focused on Jesus and the path of love and servitude to which they had been called. In contrast to their lives under the Mosaic Law, where obedience to the law defined their actions, Christianity had become a way of living, and they took it very seriously…but joyfully.

All of these things they did as a matter of honoring God. Consequently, they were smiled upon by one another, delighting in each others' company. Interestingly, they also gained favor with the community that surrounded them. Their fellow Jews saw something in these believers that they had not seen prior. They saw genuineness in them in contrast to the conceit and self-absorption of the Pharisees who were their supposed spiritual leaders.

As they continued fellowshipping and learning together, they also shared the gospel message with others. As the days and weeks passed, their fellow Jews became noticeably thirsty for something these believers had to offer. They wanted what they saw in Jesus' followers. Is it any wonder their numbers continued to grow rapidly? On a daily basis, more and more were being saved.

Luke continued relating the story of the growth and maturity of the church to Theophilus through the balance of the book of Acts. As promised, the Word of God eventually spread to many nations leaving independent congregations of Christians scattered throughout Israel, Asia Minor, and Europe. Through the efforts of the Holy Spirit and the apostles, God's ultimate goal of establishing a living, breathing body of believers would be realized – a body that came to life on the Day of Pentecost.

Chapter 11

Baptism

A book that focuses on apostolic authority would be incomplete without some examples of doctrinal diversity that originate, at least to some degree, from the way men view the events of the Day of Pentecost. While some doctrines derive from a misunderstanding of, or lack of respect for, the apostles' instructions, still others have developed because men have failed to consider the whole of New Testament teaching in order to fully understand the events of Pentecost.

One apostolic doctrine that has been treated in a rather careless fashion is the doctrine of baptism. Jesus and the apostles placed heavy emphasis on the rite of baptism throughout the whole of the New Testament, intimately linking immersion in water directly to one's salvation. Peter, Paul, and John, the three apostles responsible for the bulk of the New Testament epistles, wrote and spoke a great deal about the redemptive value of this rite.

The antecedents to baptism are seen in the Old Testament washings commanded of the Israelites under the Mosaic Law as well as the baptism performed by John the Baptist. Much of the preparation for Christian immersion is found in the books of gospel (Matthew, Mark, Luke, and John). There we learn of the purifying characteristic of baptism:

> [25] Then a matter of dispute developed on the part of John's disciples with a Jew about purification. [26] And they came to John and said to him, "Rabbi, He who was with you beyond the Jordan, to whom you have testified—behold, He is baptizing and all *the people* are coming to Him." (John 3: 25-26)

John the Baptist's disciples became jealous of Jesus and his disciples – a jealousy based upon the fact that Jesus' disciples were baptizing so many people. Interestingly, the argument concerning baptism arises out of a discussion about purification. It is not surprising that the subject of purification would focus on baptism for first century Israelites. In the Old Testament, which was the only Bible these men had, purification was often associated with the cleansing rituals commanded by God (Numbers 8: 7, 21; 19: 9; 31: 23; Ezra 6: 20). God's use of water for religious cleansing in the Abrahamic covenant was well known. Similarly, they understood that the baptism they were practicing under John's guidance was an instrument of purification.

> John the Baptist appeared in the wilderness, preaching a baptism of repentance for the forgiveness of sins. (Mark 1: 4)
>
> And he came into all the region around the Jordan, preaching a baptism of repentance for the forgiveness of sins; (Luke 3: 3)

Prior to his ascension, Jesus spent much time teaching the apostles about the things he considered most important. From his words we know that Jesus considered baptism to be a most significant doctrine since he was so emphatic about the import of baptism.

> [19] Go, therefore, and make disciples of all the nations, baptizing them in the name of the Father and the Son and the Holy Spirit, [20] teaching them to follow all that I commanded you; and behold, I am with you always, to the end of the age." (Matthew 28: 19-20)

While the command to baptize people in the process of making disciples is convincing, Jesus tied salvation to baptism according to these words found in the gospel of Mark:

> [15] And He said to them, "Go into all the world and preach the gospel to all creation. [16] The one who has believed and has been baptized will be saved; but the one who has not believed will be condemned. (Mark 16: 15-16)

Similarly, in a conversation Jesus had with a man named Nicodemus, he offered the following, defining baptism as critical for entering the kingdom of God:

> Jesus answered, "Truly, truly, I say to you, unless someone is born of water and *the* Spirit, he cannot enter the kingdom of God. (John 3: 5)

Since, upon proclamation of the gospel message, Jesus anticipated that people would believe and be baptized, we know that he considered baptism to be a primary component of that message. Jesus boldly proclaimed to his followers the redemptive role of baptism in the covenant of grace.

Early Christians understood that baptism (immersion) in water was intended for the forgiveness of sins. It was the moment of rebirth for the repentant sinner. On the Day of Pentecost, Peter told the crowd that they must be baptized as a matter of forgiveness:

> Peter *said* to them, "Repent, and each of you be baptized in the name of Jesus Christ for the forgiveness of your sins; and you will receive the gift of the Holy Spirit. (Acts 2: 38)

Peter later supplemented this teaching in his first epistle when he compared baptism to the flood of Noah's day, noting that the source of baptism's redemptive power is found in the resurrection of Jesus Christ:

> [20] ...when the patience of God kept waiting in the days of Noah, during the construction of the ark, in which a few, that is, eight persons, were brought safely through *the* water. [21] Corresponding to that, baptism now saves you—not the removal of dirt from the flesh, but an appeal to God for a good conscience—through the resurrection of Jesus Christ, (1 Peter 3: 20b-21)

The apostle Paul wrote much about the rite of baptism and the significant changes that take place at the time a person is immersed in water in Jesus' name. In his letter to the Galatians, he described a person's baptism as the moment he/she became clothed with Christ.

> For all of you who were baptized into Christ have clothed yourselves with Christ. (Galatians 3: 27)

Later, as he penned his epistle to the Romans, the apostle echoed Peter's teaching of forgiveness at the time of baptism while discussing in great depth the new life men attained once they were baptized:

> [3] Or do you not know that all of us who have been baptized into Christ Jesus have been baptized into His death? [4] Therefore we have been buried with Him through baptism into death, so that, just as Christ was raised from the dead through the glory of the Father, so we too may walk in newness of life. [5] For if we have become united with *Him* in the likeness of His death, certainly we shall also be *in the likeness* of His resurrection, [6] knowing this, that our old self was crucified with *Him*, in order that our body of sin might be done away with, so that we would no longer be slaves to sin; [7] for the one who has died is freed from sin. (Romans 6: 3-7)

These verses are but a taste of the myriad of biblical passages that deal with baptism. They paint a vivid picture of the apostolic teaching that baptism has a critical role in one's redemption. The word *baptism*, in some form, appears in the New Testament nearly one hundred times, so it is clearly something the apostles considered significant. As we have seen, during the initial presentation of the gospel message that was preached on the Day of Pentecost, baptism is portrayed as both a command from the apostles and a response of faith from the crowd (Acts 2: 37-41).

The Apostolic Fathers, men who were directly or indirectly influenced by the New Testament apostles, had much to say concerning the redemptive role of baptism in the church age. For example, in the early stages of the church The Epistle of Barnabas was believed to have been written by Barnabas, Paul's companion, although some have claimed that the letter may have been penned by either Barnabas of Alexandria or another apostolic student of the same name. Nevertheless, many of the early church fathers, attributing the work to Barnabas of Cyprus with strong conviction, considered the letter equivalent with Scripture, believing it might easily have been canonized based on its conformance to apostolic teachings. In it we read these words concerning the ceremony of baptism:

> Now let us see if the Lord has been at any pains to give us a foreshadowing of the waters of Baptism and of the cross. Regarding the former, we have the evidence of Scripture that Israel would refuse to accept the washing which confers the remission of sins and would set up a substitution of their own instead [Jer 22:13; Isa 16:1-2; 33:16-18; Psalm 1:3-6]. Observe there how he describes both the water and the cross in the same figure. His meaning is, "Blessed are those who go down into the water with their hopes set on the cross." Here he is saying that after we have stepped down into the water, burdened with sin and defilement, we come up out of it bearing fruit, with reverence in our hearts and the hope of Jesus in our souls. This He saith, because we go down into the water laden with sins and filth, and rise up from it bearing fruit in the heart, resting our fear and hope on Jesus in the spirit.[44]

An early, rather well-known student of the apostles was a man named Ignatius. We do not know exactly when he was born and when he died, although there is some evidence that he died around AD 110,

---

[44] Carlson, Steven A., Baptism and the Plan of Salvation, citing the Epistle of Barnabas, p. 305.
  Barnabas, THE EPISTLE OF BARNABAS (c. A.D. 70), (11:1-10) – While some ascribe this letter to Barnabas of Alexandria, an early church father, most scholars agree that it is the work of Paul's companion.

probably between the ages of 75 and 85. Known as Ignatius of Antioch, he studied under the apostle John and may have even done some studying under Paul. He wrote the following in <u>The Epistle of Ignatius to the Trallians:</u>

> Wherefore also, ye appear to me to live not after the manner of men, but according to Jesus Christ, who died for us, in order that, by believing in His death, ye may by baptism be made partakers of His resurrection.[45]

Numerous other quotes could be cited from various other church fathers who repeat what these have stated. Those church fathers who addressed the topic of baptism were unanimous in their teaching that the rite of immersion in water was a matter of salvation.

In modern times, the teaching of the apostles concerning baptism has been brushed aside so fully that men have come to teach, contrary to Galatians 3: 27, that even those who have *not* been baptized have clothed themselves with Christ. Faith only – the notion that men need only believe in Jesus in response to the gospel – is taught as the way to salvation. This is a teaching that developed during the Reformation Movement of the sixteenth century. Yet it is a view that conflicts with the apostolic instructions noted in this chapter.

Men and women who understand and appreciate the role of the apostles and the critical nature of their teachings should seriously reconsider what they have been told regarding apostolic instructions surrounding baptism. We have seen a concerted effort over the past five hundred years to negate the significance of baptism through arguments that make light of the apostles' doctrine. Several good books[46] are available that can not only help the earnest student of the Bible better understand the rite, but also shed some light on the theological obstacle course men have invented and chosen to navigate in an effort to skirt the lessons of the apostles regarding baptism.

---

[45] Ignatius, <u>The Epistle of Ignatius to the Trallians,</u> Chapter 2, BE SUBJECT TO THE BISHOP, ETC.

[46] G. R. Beasley-Murray, <u>Baptism in the New Testament</u>; Jack Cottrell, <u>Baptism, A Biblical Study</u>; Steven A. Carlson, <u>Baptism and the Plan of Salvation: Restoring the New Testament Gospel,</u> Steven A. Carlson, <u>Baptism and the Battle for Souls: Faith That Demands Obedience, Born of Water and the Spirit: (Entering the Kingdom,</u> Steven A. Carlson.

Chapter 12

Spiritual Gifts

Another critical misstep with respect to apostolic doctrine relates to the distribution of the miraculous spiritual gifts of the first century (e.g., speaking in tongues, healing, prophesying, etc.). Many believe and teach that these gifts were common among believers at the time and that God would distribute them at any given moment via the outpouring of the Spirit (as witnessed on the Day of Pentecost) on any believer who asked. However, this is not the picture of spiritual gifts that we find in God's Word.

Before delving into the distribution of gifts, we must consider the nature of spiritual gifts since they are so diverse. Not all spiritual gifts manifest themselves in a physically miraculous fashion. For instance, when Peter spoke of the promised "gift of the Holy Spirit" (Acts 2: 38), he did not suggest that such a gift automatically results in miraculous abilities. In this instance, the Greek word translated as *gift*,[47] is the word *dorea*, which simply means *a* (divine) *gratuity*. Lessons from other apostles describe an indwelling spiritual presence for those who have accepted Jesus as Savior.

> However, you are not in the flesh but in the Spirit, if indeed the Spirit of God dwells in you. But if anyone does not have the Spirit of Christ, he does not belong to Him. (Romans 8: 9)

> Do you not know that you are a temple of God and *that* the Spirit of God dwells in you (1 Corinthians 3: 16)

> By this we know that we remain in Him and He in us, because He has given to us of His Spirit. (1 John 4: 13)

Scholars generally agree that these passages depict the "gift of the Holy Spirit" (Acts 2: 38) mentioned in Peter's sermon on the Day of Pentecost. The Holy Spirit abides with believers as a helper and teacher (John 14: 26). However, the presence of the Spirit about which

---

[47] *1431*. δωρεα **dorea**, do-reh-ah'; from *1435*; a gratuity:--gift.Strong, James, The New Exhaustive Concordance of the Bible-Dictionary of the Greek Testament, p. 24.

these authors wrote is not the same as the manifestation of the Spirit as it is presented on the Day of Pentecost and various other times throughout the New Testament (Acts 10: 44-46; 19: 6). On those occasions the Spirit manifested himself via certain wonders such as speaking in tongues. When the apostles addressed the openly manifested gifts in Scripture, the word used to describe those gifts is the Greek word *charisma*.[48] Although the word is not always linked to them, it is often used in connection with these special gifts (1 Corinthians 14: 1, 12).

The apostle Paul spent some time in his epistles discussing spiritual gifts. He addressed the topic extensively in chapters twelve through fourteen of his first epistle to the Corinthians where these gifts were causing a rift within the church body. Also, in his letters to Timothy, Paul mentioned the fact that this young Christian had received spiritual gift(s):

> Do not neglect the spiritual gift within you, which was granted to you through *words of* prophecy with the laying on of hands by the council of elders. (1 Timothy 4: 14)

> For this reason I remind you to kindle afresh the gift of God which is in you through the laying on of my hands. (2 Timothy 1: 6)

Some may wonder if there is a difference between the kinds of gifts bestowed in these two verses. Notice that in the first instance a gift was given to Timothy when the elders laid hands on him in connection with prophecy. On the second occasion a gift was bestowed through the apostle Paul. Interestingly, the same word, *charisma*, is used to define each of these gifts.

Just as the word charisma carries different meanings, there are differing schools of thought with respect to these passages and the gift(s) Timothy received. For instance, B. W. Johnson makes the following claim concerning these remarks by Paul:

> 1 Timothy 4: 14
> *Neglect not the gift.* The allusion is to special spiritual gifts given to him to fit him for the duties of an evangelist. These were given, and were essential, in that first age. *By prophecy.* As the Spirit at Antioch said to the prophets,

---

[48] *5486*. χηαρισμα **charisma**, *khar'-is-mah*; from *5483*; a (divine) *gratuity*, i.e. *deliverance* (from danger or passion); (spec.) a (spiritual) *endowment*, i.e. (subj.) religious *qualification*, or (obj.) miraculous *faculty*:--(free) gift. Ibid, p. 77.

"Separate to me Paul and Barnabas," I suppose a revelation was given that Timothy was to be set apart, and that he would be spiritually endowed for his work. *With the laying on of hands.* He was ordained in the usual way, and at the ordination the Spirit conferred upon him new gifts. It must be borne in mind that the ancient evangelists had no New Testament to guide them, and hence needed special qualifications.[49]

2 Timothy 1: 6
Stir up the gift of God. The supernatural gift which he received by the imposition of the apostolic hands. The gift of office was conferred by the ordination at the hands of the presbytery; the gift of miraculous powers, by the imposition of the hands of an apostle.[50]

B. W. Johnson held that the elders of the church ordained Timothy for his ministry in Christ in keeping with the *religious qualification* definition of *charisma* (see page 84). He also notes the likelihood of one or more miraculous spiritual gift(s) received by Timothy through the hands of the apostle. The fact that Mr. Johnson believes miraculous spiritual gifts were distributed at the time of the ordination suggests that he believes Paul was present for that ceremony. Similarly, Matthew Henry offers the following thoughts concerning these verses:

1 Timothy 1: 14
Here see the scripture-way of ordination: it was by the laying on of hands, and the laying on of the hands of the presbytery. Observe, Timothy was ordained by men in office. It was an extraordinary gift that we read of elsewhere as being conferred on him by the laying on of Paul's hands, but he was invested in the office of the ministry by the laying on of the hands of the presbytery.[51]

2 Timothy 1: 6
He exhorts him to stir *up the gift of God* that was *in him.* Stir it up as fire under the embers. It is meant of all the gifts and graces that God had given him, to qualify him for the work of an evangelist, the gifts of the Holy Ghost, the extraordinary gifts that were conferred by the imposition of the apostle's hands.[52]

Matthew Henry echoes the thoughts of B. W. Johnson in that the laying on of hands by the elders was designed to ordain Timothy into

---

[49] Johnson, B. W., The People's New Testament with Explanatory Notes, p. 267.
[50] Ibid, p. 275.
[51] Henry, Mathew, Matthew Henry's Commentary on the Whole Bible, SearchGodsWord.org.
[52] Ibid.

the ministry of Christ. On the other hand, the gift received at Paul's hands was most likely a gift that manifested itself in some miraculous fashion, although we are not told what gift Timothy received. This truth is also recognized in *Believer's Bible Commentary* by William MacDonald.[53] A. T. Robertson has commented that this was likely an ordination that occurred at the same time that Paul bestowed a gift to Timothy, recognizing that the Greek word *meta* was used to describe the laying on of hands by the presbyters. He stated, "**meta** *does not express instrument or means, but merely accompaniment.*"[54] Thus the hands of the elders were not the instrument, but they simply accompanied Timothy's reception of a gift. Bible scholars like John Wesley,[55] John Gill,[56] and others agree. Consider these words from Jamieson, Faussett, & Brown concerning these verses:

> 1 Timothy 4: 14:
> with . . . laying on of . . . hands--So in Joshua's case (Numbers 27:18-20, Deuteronomy 34:9). The gift was connected with the symbolical act of laying on hands. But the *Greek* "with" implies that the *presbyter's* laying on hands was the mere *accompaniment* of the conferring of the gift. "By" (2 Timothy 1:6) implies that *Paul's* laying on his hands was the actual *instrument* of its being conferred. [57]
>
> 2 Timothy 1: 6
> gift of God--the spiritual grace received for his ministerial office, either at his original ordination, or at his consecration to the particular office of superintending the Ephesian Church *fearlessness, power, love, and a sound mind* (2 Timothy 1:7).
>
> by the putting on of my hands--In 1 Timothy 4:14, it is "with [not *by*] the laying on of the hands *of the presbytery.*" The apostle was chief in the ordination, and to him "BY" is applied. The presbytery were his assistants; so "with," implying merely *accompaniment,* is said of them. Paul was the instrument in Timothy's ordination and reception of the grace then conferred; the presbyters were the concurrent participants in the act of ordination; so the *Greek,* "*dia*" and "*meta.*" So in ordinations by a bishop in our days, he does the *principal* act; they join in laying on hands *with* him.[58]

---

[53] MacDonald, William, Believer's Bible Commentary, SearchGodsWord.org.
[54] Robertson, A. T., Robertson's Word Pictures, SearchGodsWord.org.
[55] Wesley, John, Wesley's Explanatory Notes, SearchGodsWord.org.
[56] Gill, John, Gill's Exposition of the Entire Bible, SearchGodsWord.org.
[57] Jamieson, Faussett, & Brown, A Commentary on the Old and New Testaments, Volume 3, p. 493.
[58] Ibid, p. 503.

Over the course of history scholars have recognized that the distribution of spiritual gifts to the members of the body of Christ in the first century was a task specific to the apostles (the twelve plus Paul). Such is the case when it comes to the gift(s) bestowed upon Timothy. As B. W. Johnson noted, the circumstances and needs of the first century church were unique in that they had no New Testament, much less the dozens of translations that have been made available over the centuries, and the apostles could spread themselves only so thin. Thus, spiritual gifts served to bind the churches together, provide for the needs of the people, and reveal God's will (through prophecy) to those who had little or no access to the apostles.

Having misunderstood, or misconstrued, the events of Pentecost, men have diminished the role of the apostles in the first century, especially with respect to the distribution of spiritual gifts. The Holy Spirit came *to* men *through* the apostles. In fact, there is no recorded incident in Scripture where such gifts were distributed outside the presence of an apostle. Normally these gifts were given through the touch of the apostles' hands (Acts 6: 6; 8: 14-18; 19: 6; Romans 1: 11). An exception to this convention occurred when the Holy Spirit fell upon the Gentiles at the house of Cornelius as a sign to Peter and the rest of the Jews (Acts 10: 44; 15: 8). Yet, even on that occasion an apostle was present.

We are told that the Corinthians received numerous spiritual gifts (1 Corinthians 12: 1-9), but the occasion when those gifts were bestowed is not revealed to us. Each time we witness the bestowal of spiritual gifts in the New Testament, at least one apostle is involved; therefore, we have every reason to believe that the Corinthians received their gifts through these men. Additionally, one reason Paul wanted to visit the Romans was so that he could distribute spiritual gifts among them (Romans 1: 11). We have no scriptural instruction that would lead us to believe that these gifts would continue beyond the time of the apostles, who were the instrument of their distribution.

In modern times, men often claim to be recipients of these special gifts, overlooking God's use of the apostles for their distribution in the first century. This stems in part from the insistence that the apostles were mere Christians and were not specially sanctioned on the Day of Pentecost as God's select messengers. Many have failed to understand or accept that the office of apostle and the extraordinary abilities accompanying that office were specific to these twelve men (plus Paul) in the first century. To many the twelve were simply *among* the more than one hundred on whom God poured out his Spirit on the Day of Pentecost. Thus, the significance of the apostolic office has, over time, been underestimated in the eyes of men in such a way that their doctrines are often criticized and discarded as though they were optional or, worse yet, as if they were wrong.

God always provides believers with the tools necessary to fulfill the tasks he has given them. That is what occurred in the early church as God delivered spiritual gifts via the apostles' touch. The miraculous gifts of the first century allowed the Christians of that day to accomplish God's will of establishing the church. The apostles were the *means* God used to bestow the gifts. Modern proclamation of the candid and spontaneous distribution of miraculous gifts of the Spirit ignores the biblical function of the apostles relative to these special gifts.

Conclusion

The misreading of the details of the Day of Pentecost has muddied the doctrine of men in that it has led many to trivialize the role of the apostles with respect to the church. If asked, many would almost certainly insist that Jesus, and only Jesus, is the foundation of the church. However, according to Scripture, that is not the case.

> [19] So then you are no longer strangers and foreigners, but you are fellow citizens with the saints, and are of God's household, [20] having been built on the foundation of the apostles and prophets, Christ Jesus Himself being the cornerstone, [21] in whom the whole building, being fitted together, is growing into a holy temple in the Lord, [22] in whom you also are being built together into a dwelling of God in the Spirit. (Ephesians 2: 19-22)

The prophets and apostles played critical roles in the development of the church of Christ. They were foundational in the establishment of the church while Jesus assumed the position of the cornerstone upon which the balance of the foundation (prophets and apostles) must rely in order to remain straight and true.

It was the role of the prophets to prepare men for Jesus' coming and ultimately prepare mankind for the covenant of grace in which we live. They offered credibility to men like John the Baptist[59] and the apostles. It was difficult for people to ignore the fulfillment of prophecies that had been offered centuries earlier.

The apostles, on the other hand, were at ground zero as the institution of the church was launched. Teaching those who would become Christ's followers was their responsibility. Therefore, the Spirit came upon these men to distinguish them as God's agents among mankind. The events of Pentecost helped others to recognize the special role of the apostles. As God's representatives, men were to receive the words spoken by the apostles as God's words. As they

---

[59] The prophet Isaiah spoke of John the Baptist when he said, *A voice is calling, "Clear the way for the LORD in the wilderness; Make smooth in the desert a highway for our God.'* (Isaiah 4: 3)

Malachi also prophesied concerning John the Baptist: *Behold, I am going to send My messenger, and he will clear the way before Me And the Lord, whom you seek, will suddenly come to His temple; and the messenger of the covenant, in whom you delight, behold, He is coming," says the LORD of hosts.* (Malachi 3: 1)

spoke, and as they wrote, the teachings of the apostles provided the doctrine of Christ by which men were to live.

By insisting that the apostles were merely *among* the believers who received the Spirit on the day of Pentecost, men have effectively, yet mistakenly, lifted the one hundred twenty disciples to a level of equality with the apostles with respect to the Day of Pentecost. However, that is in conflict with the clear objective of the first two chapters of Acts. The narrative expressly focuses on the apostles and their foundational role in the early church.

Downplaying the apostles' role on the Day of Pentecost by insisting that they were, in essence, equal with all other believers, has offered men the opportunity to make light of many of the teachings found in the New Testament, which was penned by the apostles or those under their immediate influence. A biblical teaching that someone considers unappealing may be more easily ignored or abandoned if the one who wrote it is considered *just another Christian*.

The apostles were set aside on the Day of Pentecost precisely so men would respect their foundational role and the unwavering truths they left behind. Abandoning their biblical role in the church has led many, in an often-cavalier fashion, to develop doctrines that conflict with apostolic instruction. Yet, God intended for men to abide by the doctrine of the apostles just as the early church did (Acts 2: 42).

If this lesson about the sanctioning of the apostles on the Day of Pentecost has taught us anything, it is how casually men discount and even ignore the Spirit-breathed teachings of God's Word. This has resulted in a veritable smorgasbord of beliefs strewn across Christendom that contradict one another and often conflict with the words of the apostles. We would witness considerably fewer doctrinal disputes if more men were like the Bereans of the first century.

> [10] The brothers immediately sent Paul and Silas away by night to Berea, and when they arrived, they went into the synagogue of the Jews. [11] Now these people were more noble-minded than those in Thessalonica, for they received the word with great eagerness, examining the Scriptures daily *to see* whether these things were so. (Acts 17: 10-11)

The Bereans were admired for their nobility. The reason they were respected is that they took seriously the message of the Bible, recognizing that the lessons taught by men were subordinate to, and must always be measured against, those inspired by God. Refusing to blindly accept even the teachings of Paul and Silas, the Bereans considered the words of Scripture and compared them to what these men had to say. This kind of faithfulness to biblical doctrine is no less important for us today.

The Day of Pentecost stands as a pivotal moment in the history of mankind. The outpouring of the Holy Spirit on men is no less significant than the birth of God's Son as he was sent to live among men. However, just as the Gnostics of the late first century erred concerning the divine incarnation of Jesus (1 John 2: 22-23), many men have misconstrued the events surrounding the birth of the church. This has led to certain doctrinal views that do not harmonize with God's Word.

Getting back to the basics of apostolic instruction is not an easy quest. It takes a considerable amount of effort – probably more than most are willing to exert. The journey begins when someone decides to delve into God's Word and discover for himself/herself exactly what the Bible teaches, and then gauges the words of men against the words of Scripture. It involves reading and studying what the apostles taught rather than simply accepting the interpretations of men.

Still, the prize is well worth the effort. Recognizing the apostles as God's chosen messengers and heeding their instructions is a critical step in understanding the truth of God's Word and applying that truth effectively in one's life. Revering the teachings of the apostles, whom God appointed to that unique office, ultimately honors God. Making this extra effort to honor God by learning and respecting the apostles' doctrine can make an amazing difference in one's walk with the Lord.

Bibliography

http://www.englishplus.com, accessed June 24, 2010.

Carlson, Steven A., Baptism and the Plan of Salvation, Guardian Publishing, LLC, Holt, MI, 2009.

Gill, John, Gill's Exposition of the Entire Bible, SearchGodsWord.org. Accessed, June 25, 2010.

Henry, Mathew, Matthew Henry's Commentary on the Whole Bible, SearchGodsWord.org. Accessed June 25, 2010.

Jamieson, Faussett, & Brown, A Commentary on the Old and New Testaments, Volume 3, Hendricksen Publishers, Peabody, MA, 2008.

Johnson, B. W., The People's New Testament with Explanatory Notes, Gospel Light Publishing Company, 1897.

Lilliback, Peter A., Advisory Board Chairman, 1599 Geneva Bible Restoration Project, 1599 Geneva Bible, Tolle Lege Press, White Hall, VA, 2007.

Longnecker, Richard N., The Expositor's Bible Commentary – Acts, Zondervan Publishing House, Grand Rapids, MI, 1995.

MacDonald, William, Believer's Bible Commentary, SearchGodsWord.org. Accessed June 25, 2010.

McGarvey, J. W., New Commentary on Acts, Gospel Light Publishing, Delight, AR.

Reese, Gareth L., New Testament History – Acts, Scripture Exposition Books, Moberly, MO, 2002.

Robertson, A. T., Robertson's Word Pictures, SearchGodsWord.org. Accessed June 25, 2010.

Strong, James, <u>The New Exhaustive Concordance of the Bible-Dictionary of the Hebrew Bible</u>, Thomas Nelson Publishers, Nashville, TN, 1990.

Strong, James, <u>The New Exhaustive Concordance of the Bible-Dictionary of the Greek Testament</u>, Thomas Nelson Publishers, Nashville, TN, 1990.

Wesley, John, <u>Wesley's Explanatory Notes</u>, SearchGodsWord.org. Accessed June 25, 2010.

www.ingramcontent.com/pod-product-compliance
Lightning Source LLC
Chambersburg PA
CBHW031412040426
42444CB00005B/538